JACK FROST

CAME

LAST NIGHT

Facing Loss and Finding Healing

Babs Jack

ISBN 978-0-9926116-0-6

Rose Ed Publishing
www.rose-edfoundation.org

Cover Art by Mole Middleton

Printed in Great Britain

For Grace

CONTENTS

Foreword - George Carey   7

Introduction: The Gift   9

1. Memory Lane   11
2. Childhood Past   14
3. Jack Frost   23
4. A Letter for Grace   26
5. The Making of a Memory   33
6. The Miracle Unfolds   39
7. The Rocking Chair   45
8. Strength to the Weary   53
9. Through the Valley   60
10. Best-laid Plans   68
11. Carrow Pods and Tear Jars   75
12. Perfect Timing, Elsie   88
13. Burdens and Blessings   98
14. The Invisible Mask   113
15. Go for it!   125
16. Ben   138
17. My Cup Overflows   155
18. My Huge Bag of Worries   167

19. *Grace*   183

20. *Roses on the River*   197

21. *Full Circle*   205

Postscript   211

A Final Word from the Author   214

The Rose Education Foundation   219

Foreword

It is a very long time since I have read such an honest, sensitive and compelling book. I read the manuscript in one sitting, I simply could not put it down. There were two reasons for this. The first, quite obviously, is the content. A young mother loses her baby and in her despair has to wrestle with doubt, fear, confusion and depression. Babs takes us into her journey of faith and dares to ask: 'Where is God when your faith is so cruelly dashed?'

The second reason is that this book is a delight to read. It is beautifully written and Babs uses poetry, story and verse to tell her story of what the death of Grace meant to her and how she recovered her confidence that God is in control.

Some may flick through these pages and conclude that this is book for women only. This would be a bad mistake. Although the personal story of one woman, it is the narrative of a couple working through a calamity together because Chris, her husband, shared the journey with her.

I must say Babs's story echoes the experience that my wife Eileen and I shared when we were young. We lost our first child in similar circumstances. Eileen, just 22 years of age, went two weeks over full term pregnancy. Then she was told that her baby had died in her womb. She had a tough birth knowing all the while that she was giving birth to a dead baby.

Like Babs and Chris we were not helped by the specialists at the time. The Irish nurse in an awkward yet kindly way told us that our little boy, whom we named Stephen, was with God in Limbo. That was hardly helpful! Although I saw this little beautiful baby yet Eileen didn't, he was whisked from us and laid to rest in an unknown cemetery. Every April 2nd for the last 50 years we have shed a tear for him.

This is a wonderful book which will help many couples to come to terms with the loss of a child. Babs has done us all a great service in letting others read her story. It has blessed me—I am sure it will bless others also.

George Carey
Former Archbishop of Canterbury, 1991-2002

Introduction

THE GIFT

I had often thought how strange it was that memories seemingly forgotten and buried in the past could, quite suddenly, and without invitation, sneak up on you when least expected. In a fleeting moment, not meant to last forever, our attention has been caught by a touch, a smell, or even a taste—a glimpse of something, perhaps quite ordinary, that at another time or place would not be meaningful to us at all.

And yet in that one particular, special moment our souls, minds, and hearts are offered a chance to look back.

We might call it a gift. A gift which could, if we so desired, take us on a unique journey, leading us to places and reminding us of experiences long since forgotten.

Such moments are a chance to remember those who have been special to us and who have touched our lives, at a particular time, in a way that no one else could. An experience never to be repeated in quite the same way again, bringing a smile to our lips, or a tear to our eye; touching our senses as a lighted match may touch a candle's wick, causing it immediately to burst into flame, thereby creating a shaft of light that enables us to see afresh images long since past, shaded by time and yet never really lost to us at all.

These are images which help us to unravel beauty once seen, but perhaps never fully understood until faced again with eyes that are more mature and hearts more ready to receive. A second glimpse of what once was, to be recreated in the here and now.

We all live in the real world, of course. A place, at times, of harsh reality, but also the setting in which our memories are made and stored for ever. No one can take them from us. They are a gift from God. To hold a memory in our hearts is precious. Indeed, it should never be taken for granted, but treasured. And, when the moment seems right, shared.

This book is about the sharing of such a memory.

It is the memory of our daughter, Grace. She was, and will always remain, God's gift to us. I pray that through the words of this book that gift might now be shared with others.

Our daughter Grace was not meant for this world. Yet, just before she died, I know that for one brief moment our hearts were locked in love.

We breathed as one. Then my precious child was gone.

And yet, she will forever remain, through all eternity.

No longer ours.

No longer mine.

But His.

MEMORY LANE

It was a winter's morning in late November when, had our neighbours spied us, they could have been forgiven for thinking us very strange people indeed. For there we stood at the garden gate, gazing down the long country lane which led to our village, the rural setting of our new home. 'Why so strange?' you may be wondering. Well, it was five thirty in the morning, and there we were, clad in pyjamas, coats, and slippers. We were like two excited children, watching in expectation for something truly wonderful to occur.

Well, for us it had.

We had woken that morning with the realisation that, yes, this was our own home. After twenty years of full-time Christian ministry, throughout which we had lived in rented or tied accommodation, for which we had been extremely thankful, the Lord had opened up the opportunity for us to buy our own little home.

Many friends smiled as, in answer to their question, 'So how many houses did you look at?' we responded, 'Oh, just the one.' I suppose it did seem rather strange that, having been given for the first time in our married lives the freedom actually to choose the location and house were we would live, we had not looked more extensively. For us it was simple. This was not our choice, but God's. In fact, without His intervention through the love of family and friends, and several miracles of His own, it simply could not have happened. I guess you could say we saw our home as a gift. Undeserved, but, through His grace, He had made it possible.

What a loving Father He is!

As we stood that morning outside our new home, a scene unfolded before us. Everything around was incredibly quiet and peaceful, apart from our joyful expressions to each other of how very blessed we felt. As we surveyed the scene around us, my eyes fixed on the light blanket of frost covering everything in sight. It was breathtaking. The frost hung upon the trees like nature's own decorations, fragile, and yet strong. As the gentle breeze caught the trees unawares, their beauty remained constant, sparkling like frosted jewels.

Such beauty could never be captured, even by the most gifted craftsman or artist. This was, for me, a visual reminder of God's order and power, and of his gracious and generous provision.

Life is made up of special moments, and for us this had been one of them. A gift to add to what I call my treasure-store of memories, given to me throughout my life. It had become to me a beautiful mental box. A box to be opened at will, to share with others, or to keep close to my heart.

Of course, memories can be good and bad, but I have come to see that through the power of God's love in our lives, negative images can be made positive, and tears of sorrow turned to joy. Our disappointments turned into possibilities by our Heavenly Father.

And, when suffering touches us, like a sudden storm on an otherwise clear and sunny day, as it sometimes certainly does, He is there, asking us to trust Him. One tough moment after another, He reminds us that He will not send the manna all at once, but it will come, one day at a time, to strengthen and feed us and give us the courage to put one foot in front of the other, and walk forwards. Sometimes, we step out into an uncertain world. Yet, we are never alone, for He holds our hand.

As I get older, I am more and more aware of how quickly time passes. Life seems to rush ahead at such a pace it seems hard to keep up. However, in my experience, it is so important to take time to reflect not simply on where we are going, but where we have been, so that we do not forget all that we have learned along life's journey. There is something so satisfying about reading an autobiography. Why? Because it teaches us about the richness of someone else's life. It reflects on what they have done, more than what they are hoping to do. Bound up in that is a life lived, lessons learned, and memories shared.

As I begin to reflect on my own life, memory chases memory down the road of adulthood present to childhood past. It is as if I am sitting in a car alone, and surrounded by fog. I feel apprehensive and vulnerable, when suddenly, but very gradually, the fog begins to clear, and, little by little, a picture emerges, clear and strong. Instinctively, I want to wipe the windscreen, but I wait in expectation of what will be revealed.

As the excitement mounts, my breathing quickens. It is as if I am waiting to watch a production at the theatre. The music begins, the great heavy velvet curtains rise, but the stage is covered in a mist created by the dry ice machine. I wait again, with joyous expectation, and, suddenly, the mist begins to evaporate. My patience is rewarded, and I am brought face to face with the scene before me. However, these are not now actors I see before me, but real people. These are my memories. And suddenly, and most willingly, I am a child again.

CHILDHOOD PAST

As I lay in that wonderful state of being not quite asleep, and yet not quite awake, I was aware of murmurings from downstairs. It sounded as though everyone else in our household was up, except me. I felt so snug and secure in my little bed, and even more so as the realisation hit me that it was Sunday.

No school!

Although I enjoyed school, there was something special about the whole family being together. It was a day for us—Mum, Dad, and my sister Sue—to spend as we wanted. Something I looked forward to. With this thought in mind, I felt even more content, and I snuggled down feeling cosy and cosseted, the blankets, soft, fleecy, and warm, pulled right up to my nose, with only fingertips peeping out.

It was chilly. No central heating, or double-glazing then. However, there was one thing over which I had no doubt: downstairs there would be a blazing coal fire in the hearth, which Mum or Dad would have risen early to light.

Peering out over my richly-coloured eiderdown, I surveyed the scene. My bedroom. Well, I say 'my,' but really it was 'ours,' because I shared it with my older sister, Sue. It was familiar and safe. A place of sharing and of fun; of laughter, and at times of tears. It was a place where a sister became a best friend—who, to this very day, remains just that.

I remembered thinking, as I had so many times before, how very secure I felt; as a much-loved child should. I was around eight or nine years old at the time, and, even then, as now, I relished winter.

Simple things evoked pleasure then: hearing the milk float rattling up the road, and the clink of the glass bottles on our bright red step, which Mum used to polish until it shone; hearing the laughter in Mum's voice as she scolded the birds for stealing the cream from the top of the milk again; the sound of the postman's boots on crunchy snow; musing how very fortunate I was to still be snuggled up in bed while he had been up since the crack of dawn, and wondering what surprises he may have put through the letter box, especially if it was someone's birthday; knowing that scarves gloves and boots would always be warming by the fire; the creamy taste of porridge, which Mum always insisted was good for us, and, notwithstanding our protestations of 'we're not hungry,' had a special taste only she could conjure up. On school days, we would then leave for school, all bundled up like the Michelin men, knowing that when we came home, Mum would be there to welcome us.

Yes, I relished winter even then.

To me, it offered its own warmth—even security: open coal or log fires; lights twinkling in the houses at only four o'clock; family times with my Uncle Pat and Auntie Eileen, Mum's sister and brother-in-law, and our cousin Lyn, who has remained my dearest friend these past fifty years or more.

There was bonfire night, with the smell of chestnuts roasting, and potatoes baking in their jackets, lovingly prepared by the ladies, while my Dad and Uncle, who were also best friends, prepared the actual display. Strange how everything smelled and tasted different then. Perhaps it was because we had less 'E' numbers, and more time to prepare and appreciate what we had. I enjoyed the simple pleasure of holding a sparkler, and watching with wonder at glorious displays of colour in the sky, to cries of 'oohs' and 'aahs' and 'don't hold your sparkler too close to the end.' I recall thinking to myself, 'Stop worrying, Mum,' and yet secretly feeling, even at that tender age, comforted that she did, because of the sense of love it gave.

Bonfire night was of course swiftly followed by Christmas. It was a magical time, full of busy-ness for Mum and Dad, for whom nothing was ever too much trouble as far as their family were concerned. In the run up to Christmas Eve, there was the choosing or making of gifts, each one carefully thought about for each loved individual.

For me, it was such a special occasion to visit the shops in the centre of Birmingham: feeling the crisp snow under our feet; watching the man who sold hot chestnuts and potatoes from his cart, calling out to the crowds, 'Sixpence a bag,' his breath turning into tiny patches of steam as he spoke, because it was so cold.

The windows in the large stores were spectacular. Some had themes from a pantomime. Huge moving figures, in glorious costumes, to depict the tale. Others told the story of the nativity, with life-sized animals that you felt would come to life, if only you could touch them. The streets were full of lights and the Salvation Army band could be seen and heard as they played carols.

I recall a young woman wearing a bonnet—she had rosy cheeks and a sweet smile—offering some food to what, to my young eyes, seemed to be a very scary old man in ragged dirty clothes. You could hardly see his face, as his head was swathed in a mass of old scarves, to protect him from the bitter weather, yet I glimpsed him smile at her as he shuffled quickly away. By this small act, I later came to understand, she had lived out the true meaning of Christmas. For she was sharing God's love, not only in word but also by her actions.

Then there was the choosing of the tree, and the inevitable unravelling of the fairy lights which, Dad always teased, someone during the year had tangled up on purpose. There were all the decorations to be sorted, each one lovingly protected in tissue paper, or carefully kept in boxes to protect them over the years.

Even to this day, two of my favourite tree decorations are ones that Mum gave me from her collection when I left home. They are two little plastic angels: one pink, one white, with swansdown wings—nothing like the sophisticated and beautifully-crafted items you can purchase today. To me, however, they are precious.

Every year that I remove them from their box, I remember them hanging on our tree at home when I was a little girl, and the memory gladdens my heart. As I write these words, other memories flood in. The rich smell of Christmas cake, mince pies, and sausage rolls being cooked; the stirring of the pudding, thinking, 'I wonder if I will get the half crown this year, or will uncle Harry get it again? Just how does he do that?' Nonetheless, knowing at the same time that there would somehow magically be a silver sixpence appearing for my sister and me as we searched through our pudding. Then the memory of watching with childlike astonishment as Dad set the top of the pudding on fire, and gentle blue flames danced around the freshly-picked sprig of holly perched proudly on top.

Another memory was being part of the Nativity play at school: always longing to be Mary, but never being chosen. So I settled, with pride, when asked to be the narrator or even an angel with tinsel halo and lacy wings, knowing Mum and Dad would be there to encourage me, even if I didn't always get my lines right.

And then, of course, there was Santa. Sue and I would lie in bed, listening for him on the roof, chattering away together in sheer anticipation and excitement of what the following day may bring. Would he have been? Would Mum and Dad like the gifts we had chosen for them?

Add to all this recollections of the times we heard the voices of Mum and Dad calling up to us in a light-hearted way, 'Come on now, girls. Off to sleep with you. He won't come until you're asleep, remember.' This was followed by lots of giggles and, 'All right, Mum. Goodnight.'

Nevertheless, it was only when sleep was heavy in our eyes that we would finally drift off into a deep slumber; not asking Santa for the moon, but, as children do, wishing for at least a handful of stars.

And so Christmas day arrived.

It was the birthday of Jesus.

Whilst it would be true to say that our family didn't fully understand the wonder of it at that time in our lives, we still had a level of awareness that resulted in our acknowledging it as being special, because of His coming into our world. We held a belief, however limited, that He was in fact God's Son. Quite simply, we had been taught, and believed in, the aura that surrounded the Nativity story, albeit without fully grasping the significance of what effect this tiny baby's life would have on our own in the years to come.

After Christmas, there was the coming of springtime. The onset of evenings that began to stretch out before us; bright green buds appearing on the branches of the trees, and beautiful blossoms heavy with scent all around us; baby lambs in the fields, and tiny ducklings frantically trying to keep up with their proud parents as they waddled along.

Easter-time came, and I remember pressing my nose against the shop window that had been beautifully decorated in yellows and greens, with tiny fluffy chicks, and enormous exquisitely-crafted chocolate eggs displayed for all to see. Of course, these were not bought by ordinary people like us, but were often given to charities or hospitals to distribute, as was right and proper.

Nonetheless, on Easter morning there were always wonderful eggs for my sister and me. Some would be hidden, and we would have to hunt for them; my parents enjoying our squeals of delight as we discovered their hiding places.

There was always one special egg for each of us. It was covered in thick, dark chocolate, the front decorated with delicate flowers and little yellow chicks. The egg would sit proudly in a lovely box, encircled by a brightly coloured bow, our mouths watering at the very sight of it.

These eggs were always the last to be eaten and there was always a certain feeling of sadness as these edible pieces of art were broken up and to be devoured. The sadness soon evaporated, however, as mouths were filled with the delicious chocolate. Even as I write, I can still smell its sweetness, and recall the richness and flavour of the taste.

In the spring and summer months, my uncle Pat, auntie Eileen and my cousin Lyn would join us for family outings. The two families would motor out in convoy for picnics. Once we arrived at our destination, the two men—the dearest of friends—loved nothing more than to rush ahead to hide, before jumping out on their women and children at the most unexpected places, reducing us all to helpless laughter.

My uncle Pat was particularly fond of impersonating monkey antics at such times, and we would laugh so much, our sides literally ached. I will never forget those times together.

They were, in fact, priceless.

Finally, in my trip down memory lane, I am transported back to the little sweet shop which my parents owned. It is Christmas again and frosty outside. As I watch them working alongside each other, the little bell on the door rings as a mother and her children enter the shop. While chatting warmly to their customers, Dad breaks up the toffee they have asked for with a little silver hammer, and puts it in home-made greaseproof bags shaped like cones—a little extra on the top. Well, it is Christmas. Mum counts out the pink and white sugar mice and gently places them in a box lined with tissue paper, giving the children a free stripy candy cane as they wait patiently at their mother's side. A generous act, so typical of my parents.

Last year, I walked into an old-fashioned sweet shop. As soon as I heard the sound of the tinkling bell on the door, I was whisked back, in my mind, and could hear the silver hammer cracking the toffee, and smelled its sweetness. I could see the sugar mice on the shelves. Every fibre of my being wanted, just for that moment, to be back in the security of my parents' shop and to feel their arms around me, a child again.

So where had these all-important memories come from?

Ian Woodroffe employs a helpful metaphor, introduced in the title of his book *The Invisible Suitcase*. As I was writing down my own memories, I was reminded that we all carry with us our own 'invisible suitcase,' from which we cannot detach ourselves. It is with us all of our lives, regardless of age. It packs itself, and we have no real control over the process. It opens itself at will, and we usually have no control over where and when it opens.

The material in our suitcase is divided, Woodroffe suggests, into three categories. Firstly, factual information, such as the date of the battle of Hastings etc. Then, facts and emotions, where the fact and emotion are inseparable, such as recalling an anniversary that is centred on a date and noticing what feelings we experience when we recall that date. Finally, we have emotions, or 'free floating emotions,' which are not consciously attached to any fact or event, and which may surface at any time, sometimes engulfing us with emotions we thought had long since been forgotten—just as hearing a tinkling bell in an old-fashioned sweet shop transported me back home to a place of safety and love.

Such moments can act as restorative points in our lives, especially when we are facing our toughest times.

Quite recently, my cousin Lyn and her younger sister Jo reminded me of some of the invisible suitcase moments that at different times had been precious to them both.

Jo was only five years old when her Dad, my uncle Pat, tragically died. Lyn was ten years older, and my dearest friend. My Uncle Pat was a wonderful man, married to my Mum's sister Eileen. The death of my dear uncle was tragic, not least to my Dad, as he and Pat were best mates, as well as brothers-in-law.

They say that when you lose a child you lose part of your future, and when you lose a parent you lose part of your past. My heart ached for my cousins as I saw their sadness. After all, I still had my Dad, and it was hard, at fifteen, to know how to support them.

My parents lived in Weston-Super-Mare, in Somerset, and were very close to my Auntie Eileen and my cousins. Jo still remembers the occasions she came to visit my parents from Birmingham, and how her Uncle Tom, my Dad, told her lots of stories about a character called Fairy Cucumber, who had wonderful adventures.

As we were reminiscing together recently, she recalled how one evening Dad took us for fish and chips on the beach. Sitting in his big blue car, on the cream leather seats that seemed huge to her as a little girl, we sat and ate our fish and chips while looking out to sea. As we ate, chatting away, Dad related to Jo that Fairy Cucumber thought she was a special little girl. She had seen her picking wild flowers and grasses for her Auntie Kay, which was a very kind thing to do.

In recounting this, Jo laughed as she recollected how her poor auntie would have every vase in the house filled with grasses and wild flowers by the end of their holiday, yet she never seemed to mind. Jo then reflected that even now, as an adult and mother of three grown-up boys of her own, she had remembered that memory as if it were yesterday. She still recalled the sinking feeling when the time came for those days to end.

Then Jo added—and this is the crucial thing—'It hasn't ended. Because whenever I look at wild flowers or grasses, and think of those times with my Uncle Tom, I am that special little girl again.'

Lyn was fifteen when her Dad died, at only forty-four. She too has specific memories of Fairy Cucumber that are special to her. She vividly remembers her walks with my Dad as a little girl, while listening to his stories. She recalls the scent of lavender, white clouds scudding across the blue skies, and laughter when my Dad would break off from his tales with, 'Oh, watch out. Mind the steps!' They would then bend their knees to descend an imaginary staircase, pausing only to straighten out, and then climb back up again. Eventually, after a lot of giggling on Lyn's part, they would level out again, and the stories would continue.

Lyn once shared with me that although my Dad would not have realised how important those walks and stories were to her, she was thankful for the joy they had given to her, both then and now. She went on to observe that those times with my Dad, and his stories, act as restorative points in her memory, taking her out of the everyday, back to a time where childhood felt safe and secure. They are restorative points that have replaced negative memories in her life with positive ones.

Memories that bless rather than burn.

I have chosen just a few memories from childhood to try to illustrate how important our store of special memories and moments are to us. They are, after all, a part of our unique history; a part of who we are. They can teach us. Not in order to allow our past to dictate our future, but nonetheless to let it be a part of who we will become.

JACK FROST

Jack Frost came last night,
And light of foot and finger, as an angel in flight
Rested on my windowpane,
Leaving his signature clear and plain.
Frosted snow-flaked beauty, transcendent and frail,
Delicate as a fairy-trail.
Such fragile beauty not long to see,
As the sun shall rise, the morn to free.

Through the joy of warmth in this new day,
The wondrous image melts away.
Yet as the sunlight glistens through,
The image offers blessings new.
Beauty once seen will not depart,
But remain forever in my heart.

Yes, indeed. As a child, as far as I was concerned summer was great, but winter was special. As I lay wondering whether to get up or remain in bed, I could see a shaft of light through a chink in the curtain and decided that it must be a nice day, and probably worth getting up for.

As I mentioned earlier, Sundays were a family time and, whilst in the middle of wondering what Mum and Dad had in store for us, I heard the familiar creaking on the stairs. Dad was on his way up. Within seconds, there was a gentle knock on the door. 'Come in,' I answered in reply to his knock. The next moment my Dad was in the room. 'Good morning, sleepy head. Shall I draw the curtains?' 'Yes, please,' I replied. And with a swish of floral cloth the light poured into our room, changing its image and colours as only sunlight can.

Dad turned and smiled. 'Jack Frost came last night,' he said. Simple words, yet I was to be reminded of them many years later.

After looking out of the window for what seemed to be a long time, he turned, and came and sat on the edge of the bed where my sister and I both remained, looking at the evidence that, yes indeed, Jack Frost had paid us a visit during the night. His handiwork was there for all to see. It was as if an artist had spent hours fashioning the picture that was before us. As a spider patiently weaves its web, so a fragile, yet beautiful, picture had been created for us. The picture was of frozen snowflakes. Every one different. It was like frosted icing on a birthday cake, except no human hand could have created this scene.

As the sun began to glisten through, it appeared to enhance the beauty of the picture unfolding before us. The rays of the sun added sparkle and brought the whole magical scene to life. We began to feel the warmth of the sunshine as it filled the room, changing the picture ever so slightly from one facet of beauty to another. The warmth was welcome on such a cold day.

Jack was clever indeed—a true artist, sent to us in the middle of winter to add touches of fragile beauty to our world. How glad I was to hold on to the memory of that picture, because as the sun's rays became stronger, the sharpness of the picture began to fade, becoming distorted, and finally melting away completely, leaving only smears on the glass where a beautiful impression had been, only seconds before. I remember feeling that once gone, it was gone forever, never to be repeated.

As I shared my thoughts with Dad, he taught me a valuable lesson, which I was to draw on many years later. 'It is simple, really,' he explained. 'For you and I to have felt and appreciated the warmth and brightness of the sunshine, we had to lose the beauty of our frosted picture.' God had concealed one blessing in order to share with us another. However, the memory of it remained. Perhaps not in its entirety. But I had captured the very essence of it in my soul.

I wrote the poem above as a reminder that blessings once given remain with us forever. Now, there would be a place for a new picture to emerge. Perhaps, who knows, even more precious than the last.

Sometimes, in saying goodbye to something, or, in the case of our daughter Grace, someone, very precious, God gives us a different picture from the one we expected. A different blessing, which He asks us to share with others. We don't always understand why, except that a gift should never be held on to, but given freely and with a full heart.

A Letter for Grace

Tiny child so loved, so wanted,
Only knew her mother's womb.
Gentle little heart, still beating,
In His arms united soon.

My dearest child,

Before I begin to tell your story, I wanted to write to you, to try to express the thoughts that are in my heart right now. As I do so, I wonder if one day there may be other Mums like me that in the reading of it will understand, and feel the words echoing and resounding within their own hearts and experience.

I find it strange to think that, as I sit here alone, writing to you, there are in fact so many others who have travelled this path with me. I do not know them. And yet we each share a story that, whilst quite unique, is in so many ways the same. For we have known and understood what it is to hold a child in our hearts, yet to have been denied the joy of holding that child in our arms. Each one of us has had to say 'Goodbye,' without even being able to say 'Hello.'

For each of us, however, love remains. Also, the joy of knowing that our child was there, though perhaps only for a little while, means that we have been given the privilege of being a mother. Our baby has given us that priceless gift to hold on to forever.

As for you, Grace, you were cherished from the day I knew of your existence. Loved from conception. For a short while, you were our secret. Then came the joy of revealing our secret, our good news, to those we loved. Especially your little sister, Katie. What delight there was in the news of your coming into our lives. The thrill of sharing with close friends and family. If only you could have seen the expressions of pure joy and excitement on their faces.

For, even then, we all loved you.

As my tummy began to get rounder, I was so proud when people stopped to ask with great excitement, 'When is the baby due? What would you like?' I was thrilled. Of course, in those days, you simply had to wait and see. There was no way of knowing your gender beforehand. We had to be content with a wonderful surprise. That was fine, because we really didn't mind. So often we could be heard to comment, 'As long as it's healthy. That's all that matters.'

How I had cause to think upon those words later on. For to hold a beautiful and healthy baby in your arms, whatever the gender, is a priceless gift. 'As long as our child is safe and well,' is what we said—and we really meant it.

For you were loved unconditionally, right from the start.

There was so much joy in preparing for your coming. There was the nursery to decorate and items to be got down from the loft. The lovely, special things that your little sister Katie had used—had they been appropriate, of course. There was the lovely Moses basket that we had bought whilst in France, covered with baby animals in gentle pastel shades. And the rabbit with the floppy ears and doleful eyes that simply cried out to be loved by you. Then there was the clicking of knitting needles by your adopted 'aunties' in the church, as mountains of tiny matinee jackets and bootees were made.

In addition to all of this was the general feeling of pleasure and wellbeing generated once our good news had spread. Of course, the rest of your family couldn't wait to get to know you. Grandparents, aunties, uncles, cousins. How you would have loved them all, and they you in return.

Yet, be assured, little one. You had their love.

And that is certain, and, indeed, secure forever.

Katie was delighted at the exciting possibility of 'helping' Mummy. Although still so very little, she seemed to catch the joy of what both Daddy and I were experiencing, as, every so often, we would smile at one another, thrilled at the prospect before us. As for your Daddy, well, it goes without saying how he felt about you, right from the start. As with your sister, whom he simply adores, he was overjoyed that you were on the way.

I feel that you would be pleased to know that he participated in all aspects of parenthood, including the grubby bits, the crying bits, the sleepless nights, and so on. On hearing the news about you, I guess you could say his joy was complete. You had made him an extremely happy man, and very proud father-to-be indeed.

Although my pregnancy was not easy, the sheer joy of looking forward to you entering our world made it all worthwhile. Never for a moment did I doubt that your coming would add much richness to our lives. In that, at least, I was right—although the richness came in a way I did not expect, or could have been prepared for.

I am reminded that God only gives us the strength we need for each new day as it arrives, enabling us to cope with issues we may think are impossible to deal with at the time. We may bend as a branch in the wind. However, we need not fear. We will not break, for He holds us. The wind may rage around us, but He gives us the strength to withstand it.

I remember the story of Dorothy in *The Wizard of Oz*, a film your sister loved. Dorothy was a little girl who was suddenly, and most unexpectedly, lifted up in a tornado and carried from the security of her home in Kansas, only to be set down in a magical land with a yellow brick road. That road was to lead her to all sorts of new adventures and wonderful challenges: some pleasant, some terrifying. Finally, it was to lead her to a place of safety and the way back home. She did not walk the path alone but met friends along the way, to love and support her when, on many an occasion, she became discouraged.

Of course, that was simply a lovely children's story. Yet it reminds me that sometimes God allows us to be lifted up and carried from where we think is a safe place, setting us in the very centre of the storm. But then, He gently puts us down on a new path that takes us down a different road from the one we had expected, or desired. In so doing, He opens up along the way new possibilities and, with them, new hope.

The beauty of God's promise in Isaiah 43:5 is that He says to us, 'Do not be afraid, for I am with you.' Through loving you, dear Grace, but also through having to let you go, we have come to understand the truth and comfort of His words. What He is affirming is that He doesn't simply watch us on our journey, but travels it with us.

As Dorothy experienced on the yellow brick road, to know we are not alone helps us to face even the most tragic of situations. For us, our support came from the Lord as He walked with us every step of the way. I remember how, at the beginning of the film, the picture is in black and white. However, after Dorothy entered her new land, the images change to full colour. That, of course, is the magic of cinema, and a good director. Yet I have found that as I journey through life, at times feeling it has become very stark, due to my particular circumstances, God can restore the colour, and make life worth living again.

You see, Grace, I was never to experience the happiness of doing all the things with you that we had talked and dreamed of. For you would never discover the beautiful world that I had told you about: to smell the fragrance of a rose, experience the wind on your face, or the joy of fashioning and throwing a snowball.

You died without experiencing all that life can hold, both good and bad. You died without knowing your family and the sweetest joy that friendship can bring. However, you did not die without knowing a sense of being loved. For that was our gift to you, to hold and take with you into eternity and into the arms of a Heavenly Father who was waiting for you there.

We felt our hearts would break when we had to let you go. But God gently taught us that loving you was worth the pain. We realise, in fact, that the pain then is part of the happiness now.

Your Grandma Jack loves to do jigsaw puzzles. When I look at the picture on the box, and then at the hundreds of broken pieces on the board, I think, 'How does she have the patience to put them all together?' The wonder of it is that God sees the broken pieces of our lives yet tenderly and patiently puts them back together, revealing a picture of Himself which can only be reflected to others through the brokenness, and then the healing and restoration, in the lives of His children.

> *This heart of mine is such a fragile thing.*
> *Like fine porcelain I could set it on a shelf.*
> *But I tend to put it rather in the midst of life.*
> *Thus it has broken a million times.*
> *Perhaps the glue with which God mends it*
> *Is stronger than the stuff of which it is made.*

(Barbara Johnson, *Christian Art*)

Through the telling of your story, you will not have died in vain.

My prayer is that as it is heard, or read, you might reach into the hearts of others, who, perhaps like us, wished they had done things differently at the time.

My hope is that your story might remind them that it is never too late to grieve.

Never too late to say goodbye.

Never too late to perform an act of love.

And I hope, too, that it might be a source of assurance

for them that we can experience healing, even from what may have been the saddest moments in our lives. For the way forward is not living in the past, but allowing the past to walk with us side by side, through the issues that cause us pain, and finding a peace that we never thought possible.

There are so many things that I wanted to share with you. So many 'if onlys.' And yet, to have loved you so dearly for those nine short months, and beyond, has given me a gift that was worth all the pain, the tears, and the heartache.

I have been given a daughter called Grace.

You have blessed my life, and I am grateful.

I wrote this poem for you. In spite of the fact that we will actually never have these moments together, I know that we have shared a love that will forever remain . . . ours.

IF ONLY

If only I could hold you in my arms for just a while,
and look into those gentle eyes and see a sunny smile.
If only I could stroke your hair, feel your breath upon my cheek,
and hear you chuckle with delight as I tickle hands and feet.
If only I could feel your fingers wrapped around my own,
and promise you in gentle tones you'd never be alone.
If only I could hug you, feel your arms around so tight,
and tell your favourite stories, and sing to you at night.

If only I could listen as you giggled playfully,
and watch you as you cuddled up on Nan or Grand Pop's knee.
If only friends and family could come and visit us,
to celebrate your milestones and to make a lot of fuss.
If only, with your siblings, I could watch your friendships grow,
and know they'd share some secrets no one else would ever know.
If only I could look forward to a special family scene,
and hear you calling, 'Mummy, Daddy. Look, Santa Claus has been.'

If only it were possible to take you to a store,
and buy you nothing sensible, because that would be a bore.
Some pretty clothes, and silly toys, as frivolous as could be;
the fun would be in choosing, together you and me.
If only I could watch the story of your life unfold,
and love you, and protect you, until I'm very old.
If only there was one more hour to spend with you, I know
I'd hold the memory in my heart and never let it go.

'If onlys' were not possible, for when the angels came,
we knew that in our daughter, Grace, our loss was heaven's gain.
Yet, not even for one moment, through our grief, and tears, and sighs,
could we doubt for just one second how much you have touched our lives
We never held or saw you, yet a love so deep remains.
You came to us, you touched our lives. And we will never be the same.

5

THE MAKING OF A MEMORY

It was a most glorious day. The sun was warm on my face and as I walked along the lane, I caught the fragrant smell of blossom on the trees.

It's strange when you hold a secret in your heart. How you suspect everyone around you should know about it, and understand why it is that you are walking around with a huge smile on your face. I felt as though I was wrapped in a warm glow from head to foot. You see, I had just been given the wonderful news that I was expecting our second baby. I wanted to skip the whole way home, but realised this may be a little undignified for a minister's wife of a certain age, a supposedly sensible mother of two.

Mother of two.

How wonderful it sounded.

My heart was certainly skipping, even if my feet stayed firmly on the ground. I simply couldn't wait to get home and tell my husband, Chris, and of course our little daughter, Katie, that before long there would be another little Jack in our midst.

We were in our fourth year of marriage, and we were living in Weston-Super-Mare, in Somerset, where Chris was the Pastor of a small Evangelical Church. We had moved there after having begun our married life together in Central France, engaged in church planting with the European Christian Mission.

Katie was in her second year, and the joy of our hearts. The very thought of another blessing in our lives like Katie, or 'Daisy' as is her nickname, filled us with complete and utter joy. God had been so good to us and I, for one, was very grateful.

I simply could not imagine how it would be.

The complete joy we had received through knowing our little daughter could not be measured. She was our little treasure-store. Every new day of knowing her was more special than the last. From going into her brightly-coloured little bedroom in the morning, and watching her open her enormous blue eyes, to the feeling of utter pleasure as her tiny arms reached out to us. Then came the smiles, which would simply melt our hearts. I could never forget how secure it would feel when her little arms would tightly wrap around my neck and I would remember again that she was ours.

Having Katie had taught us new things about love. I shall never forget the feeling after giving birth. I was back in the ward and had dozed off to sleep. I remember waking up suddenly and hearing a baby crying in the nursery, which was down the corridor. Absolutely certain it was Katie, I was consumed with a love that was quite overpowering. This was something I had never experienced in quite the same way before, or since. I was a mother—and the feeling was indeed awesome.

Suddenly, there sprang up within me the overwhelming need to protect. Before I knew it, I was shuffling down the corridor and into the nursery. The midwife was there, picking up the crying infant as I arrived. Katie, however, was lying peacefully in her little crib. The midwife smiled as I stammered, now feeling a little foolish, 'I thought it might be mine.' She laughed, assuring me that 'mine' was sound asleep.

I looked into the crib and as I held that fragile, little hand, I knew I would always seek to do my very best to protect her. Forever.

My heart was filled with an indescribable love.

I was later to realise that we can't always protect our children. Not even with the deepest love.

Some things are beyond even the most loving parental control. God, however, always remains. He is there in the times we cannot be. When situations arise over which we have no power or control, He steps in on our behalf and bears the suffering for us.

As I continued my walk home on that special day, my pregnancy confirmed, my thoughts returned to when I had been pregnant with Katie and to some of the good advice that I had been given by Mums who had been there before me.

One piece of wisdom that came to mind was to make the most of every day. Because, before you know it, they are gone. I endeavoured to put this advice into action, without fully realising the full significance of it until some time later. Neither, I hasten to add, did I always achieve that ideal, however passionately I believed in it.

It is a fact that life speeds by at a rate of knots. Before we know it, our children are packing their belongings into boxes and are off to university, or wherever it is they have chosen to take that all-important next step. Somehow, without us noticing, and yet before our very eyes, our babies have become adults.

And there is a big new world waiting to be discovered.

Time spent with our children is never lost to us. It can be recalled again and again. Memories of those early years remain with us, as a constant friend with whom we walk through life's journey, hand in hand.

Such moments can only exist, however, when we give them roots and room in our lives and do not allow unnecessary things to get in the way. Things that at the time can seem so all-important, yet which may later cause us to look back with regret.

All of a sudden, those sad words, 'if only,' are on our lips.

Some time ago, I came upon a little poem that sums up this point so well.

I hope my children look back on today,
and see a parent who had time to play.
There'll be plenty of time for cleaning, and cooking.
But children grow up when we are not looking.
So quiet now cobwebs. Dust go to sleep.
I'm playing with my babies, and babies don't keep.

(Anon)

Yes, every day is special.

Every day, every minute, every breath is truly a gift.

Whether our children take big steps or little ones, achieve large things or small, each experience is to be valued and cherished as unique and precious. They are to be shared, to be laughed over, or perhaps even cried over. You see, they belong to them, and therefore are a part of us.

In the back of my Bible, I have a little scrap of paper. It is quite crumpled and worn. Brown, now, with age, since I have had it for twenty years or more and have read and re-read it time and again. Let me share it with you.

A few years ago my wife and I were travelling alone in Europe for a whole month. When we finally arrived in Rome, we had lots of letters waiting for us from my secretary, my mother, and the children. Naturally, we opened the children's mail first. The four-year old had written all the words he knew how to spell: momma, papa, uncle, cat, horse, cow. Of course, it wasn't a real letter, but it was the best he could do, and we were ecstatic. 'Look at this!' we said to each other. 'How wonderful.'

The next letter was from our three year old, who did not know how to write, so had drawn a picture of a wedding: the bride, the groom, and I was the pastor. 'Look what he has done!' we exclaimed together. We were laughing and exulting and feeling so homesick to see them.

*Then we got to the little wrinkled paper from the youngest,
who was eighteen months. It was a scribble! 'Look at this!' I
shouted. My wife started to cry, and soon I was crying.*

*The Italian pastor who had brought us the mail just
stared at us. I shoved the pieces of paper in front of his face.
'Aren't they wonderful?'*

Why didn't he respond as we had?

Because these were not his children.

*As far as my wife and I were concerned, they were the
most precious pieces of paper in the world.*

(Anon)

Quite. What would appear to be only a scribble to a stranger
is acknowledged as a triumph in the hearts of loving parents.
Every step our child takes is to be valued, for they will never
take it in quite the same way again. How sad it would be if
we were simply too busy to notice.

When Neil Armstrong reached the moon, it took just one
simple step to make his whole wonderful journey
worthwhile, and the watching world witnessed that
momentous occasion, courtesy of their television screens.

So it is with the lives of our children. Every step should
be seen as a special occasion, to be shared, and valued, and
used—never wasted. Of course, it's unlikely that the eyes of
the world will be watching! But, then, who knows?

Wouldn't it be sad, when the time came for our children
to step out onto their own particular moon, if we didn't take
the time to notice?

It has been said, in relation to that amazing journey into
space, that the real miracle lies not in the fact that man has
walked on the moon, but that, in the person of Jesus Christ,
God walked on the earth. The miracle to me is that it is this
same God and Heavenly Father who is our example. He
who cares enough about His children to notice our every
step: guiding, protecting, loving, encouraging.

Never asleep.

Never too busy.

Never disinterested.

And with every step accounted for.

What a goal for us as earthly parents to at least aim for, and thereafter to treasure forever.

It is so easy to become consumed with, 'I cant wait until they are walking.' 'Won't it be fantastic when they say their first word?' 'Just imagine their first day at school.' Of course, these are natural enough comments that, as parents, we have probably all made at one time or another. The fact remains, however, that every day in the lives of our children is special, and will never be repeated in quite the same way again.

So make the most of it.

One thing was certain. We were going to make the most of telling the people that loved us it was official. The Jacks were pregnant.

The making of a miracle had begun.

And so, too, the creating of this story.

6

THE MIRACLE UNFOLDS

Of course, the making of anything doesn't always go smoothly, or, indeed, to plan. And the making of our little miracle was no different. Most of the early months of carrying Grace were spent with my head unceremoniously down the toilet. There were a few well-meaning friends who had clearly long since passed this stage and had seemingly forgotten the joys of morning, afternoon, and evening sickness, for they would affirm, with complete sincerity, 'It's different being sick when you're pregnant, isn't it? There is something wonderful about it.'

Thankfully, that particular wonderful experience only lasted for sixteen weeks, and you will be pleased to know, I'm sure, that I myself am careful not to pass on the same words of encouragement so generously imparted to me.

What was true, however, was the 'something wonderful' part. I had been working as a midwife in our local maternity unit before becoming pregnant again, and, once I began to feel better, I continued to work for a few hours a week. It was lovely for me, working with the mums-to-be and also being pregnant myself, catching one another's joy at times. Without even a word being spoken we had a common bond in the shared excitement over all that was to come. Although I couldn't possibly have known it at the time, it was preparing me in a way for the support and empathy that I was able to offer to others at a later date.

The true 'something wonderful' came at around my seventeenth week of pregnancy. I was taking the blood pressure of a mum in the later stages of labour and suddenly felt our baby move for the first time. With Katie, I wasn't quite as certain until she'd attempted several goes at good firm kicks, but with this baby there was no doubt. Suddenly, there were tears in my eyes.

I was overwhelmed.

It seemed to make everything real.

I explained, and then apologised to the mum who was my patient. Her name was Violet, and I shall never forget the response of that lovely African lady to me. As she held on to her husband's hand, she gave me a great smile. 'I says it every time to Winston—and we've had five—when you feel it move for the first time it's the miracle unfolding. One of our babies was born dead, but I felt him move within me just once. It's all I had, but he was a miracle from God, nonetheless.'

A miracle from God, nonetheless.

How true.

Yet we sometimes feel overwhelmed by our circumstances—even angry with the One who loves us most. And then, the weight and the guilt of such feelings sweep over us. The Bible tells us so very clearly, through the words of Job, who lost everything he held dear, 'The Lord gave and the Lord has taken away. Blessed be the name of the Lord.' However, this was Job. A very godly man. An Old Testament saint. It was different for him, wasn't it?

How often we can look at such people and think that because their stories are recorded in the Bible, they had extra special powers and strengths to carry them through those painful times. But actually they were just as you and I: human, and likely to fall. So when our toe catches the edge of the hurdle, and we find ourselves hurtling face-forward onto the hard ground, how can we bless the Lord at such times? Is it possible?

In her book, *The Hiding Place*, Corrie Ten Boom recounts a poignant incident that is relevant to these questions. At one point, imprisoned in Ravensbrück concentration camp, she became so despondent—and even angry—with God, that she wondered how he could possibly be in such a place where there was so much darkness, hatred, and evil.

As I read the response from her sister, Betsy, I remember weeping openly, for she uttered these words with absolute confidence: 'There is no pit so deep, that God's love is not deeper still.' Those words are a constant reminder to me that God's shoulders are strong and broad. He understands our whys, our whining, our fears and doubting. He sees us in the terrible darkness of the pit we sometimes find ourselves in, and He understands because He has been there. Jesus—God incarnate—journeyed to the depths alone, feeling at one point in His terrible ordeal that even His Father had forsaken Him.

Chris and I had the privilege, some years ago, of visiting Oberammergau, in Bavaria, to attend the Passion Play which is held every ten years in that village. As the story of the passion unfolded, from Palm Sunday through to the resurrection of Jesus, there were so many moments of absolute wonder and amazement, and we were reminded so graphically of God's love and sacrifice on our behalf.

The portrayal of Jesus crying out to His Father, 'My God, my God, why have you forsaken me?' was so powerful that I was caused to reflect once again how Jesus suffered on the cross. He knew what it was to feel that He was without the love and support of His Father. Remember how, in the garden of Gethsemane, He pleaded that the cup of sorrow might pass Him by. Yet He added, in submission to the Father, 'Not my will, but yours be done.'

We cannot begin to understand the utter isolation Jesus felt. He faced the pit alone; something we will never have to do. For when we cry out, God will answer. Of that there is no doubt. And in His answering us in whatever circumstances we find ourselves, we can be certain of one thing. He understands.

Miracles unfold in all shapes and sizes. God's love for us cannot be measured in time or space. Yet, when we are in the darkness of the pit, and feel our hand in His, we know what has happened. For this is faith. This is about our relationship with God. This is real.

I once heard a lovely Christian Dad telling a story about his little son who was severely disabled. He could neither speak nor hear. At night, his Dad would sit by his son's cot and, in the darkness, would feel his little boy's fingers reaching out through the bars, making sure Daddy was still there until he fell asleep.

Father and son could not communicate with words, but that simple touch said it all. 'Are you still there, Daddy?' 'Yes, son, I'm still here in the darkness, so don't be afraid.' I was to learn later that sometimes our grief carries too much pain to communicate with words. At such times, we can simply reach out our hand in the darkness and we will find Him there: the God of Calvary.

As my pregnancy progressed, it felt as though life simply didn't get any better than this. I was experiencing a deep sense of well-being and feeling really healthy as I headed for the third trimester of my pregnancy. I continued to work as a midwife, which I loved. Chris and Katie were well, and life was sweet.

My earlier pregnancy with Katie had gone perfectly to plan, after the joys of feeling sick had subsided. All had progressed happily, even to Katie's grand arrival which happened exactly on her due date. I shall never forget being woken up at six a.m. on that day and feeling my first contraction. I experienced a mixture of emotions: excitement, anticipation, and thinking to myself, 'No, it can't be!' I remember waking Chris and him asking, 'Are you sure?' Well, the answer to that was, 'No.' It wasn't too long, however, before I was.

We were living in France at the time I was carrying Katie, but for various practical reasons had needed to return to England for the birth. It was lovely to be staying with my parents. Mum and Dad were wonderful, as always, offering support when needed, but allowing us our own space as well.

It was a glorious August day, and I went through most of my labour sitting in the beautiful English garden at my parents' home in Somerset. As things progressed, I was admitted into the local hospital and before long had a normal delivery.

I remember being too shaky to hold Katie immediately, so the midwife handed her to Chris first. I wouldn't have missed that moment for anything as I caught the look of inexplicable joy and wonder on his face. Even now, I can remember thinking that if I had nothing else in life I was the most blessed of all people.

We had a daughter.

We two had become three.

And I thanked God with my whole being for the gift he had given us that day.

Following that very straightforward experience, Chris and I had absolutely no reason to believe this second pregnancy, and birth, was going to be any different at all. In fact, we had only the glorious anticipation of all that was to come. It was now time to give up work and concentrate on the matter in hand: 'Operation Baby Jack Two.'

I wanted to make the most of the next few months.

There was such a joy surrounding this pregnancy. Any thoughts that with the second child there might not be quite the same level of excitement as first time around could not have been further from the truth. Everyone seemed to join in our happiness. The feeling inside me, could it have been bottled, could never have been sold—it was priceless indeed!

One of our greatest pleasures was sharing the prospect of this new life with Katie. Though still very young herself, we wanted very much to include her in our joy and for her to be able to experience something of it. Katie thought it was simply hysterical when she would place tiny items on my tummy, only to watch her active brother or sister swiftly kick them off, as if to order, to hoots of laughter from us all. I talked to her of helping Mummy with our new little one, even then relishing the prospect of fun and giggles at bath times and in so many other simple things.

My mind raced ahead to all the precious things that my children might share together in the years ahead, even as my own sister and I had done. Things that build relationships, forming ties that cannot be broken. Things that begin at childhood and last for a lifetime.

Yes, the baby was already so much a part of our lives. And the best was yet to come. We included Katie in our excitement, not for one minute wanting her to feel left out. We helped her to choose the floppy-eared rabbit with the doleful eyes that was to be her first gift to her new brother or sister.

It was as if, unknowingly, we had begun to store up for her memories of a sister she would never know, yet would be able in some small way to feel had been a part of her life. There was so much joy at that time. I am so glad that in life we cannot always see what is around the corner, for such sadness would rob us of joy in the here and now that cannot be taken away once it has been experienced.

God gives us the grace and the provision required for each and every day. Not before, but as we need it. Just as he did with the Israelites. Every day, as they needed food in the wilderness, so the manna was provided to feed them. It could not be stored up. It had to be used, or it perished. Every day, they needed to trust Him afresh. And every day the manna came.

We need not fear what may lie ahead of us. Whatever the challenges, He will help us meet them. I am reminded that manna comes in many forms, whilst the God who creates it remains the same.

❊ 7 ❊

THE ROCKING CHAIR

Christmas was just around the corner. Or so it seemed. As I noted earlier, I loved this time of year and was usually very organised. Nevertheless, this year I was struggling to keep up. When it seemed like every one else had decorations displayed, trees trimmed, and gifts neatly wrapped beneath them, I was still at the list-writing stage. But, 'Hey,' I thought to myself, 'by the time Santa takes off, I'll be ready, for sure.'

One Saturday, Chris and I left Katie with her grandparents, and we headed for the shops. After having a cup of coffee, and the largest sticky bun we could find, we decided to split up, with appropriate lists in hand, and meet up again for the nice lunch Chris had promised me.

I was eating for two, after all.

Well, that was my excuse, anyway!

As I wandered around, glancing here and there at decorated shops with all manner of gifts to buy, I drifted into an old-fashioned toyshop. It was a wonderland for children, and I most definitely began to get in touch with the child within. I couldn't wait to purchase something special for Katie. Suddenly, my attention was caught by the sound of a child's voice singing 'Twinkle, twinkle, little star.'

I was intrigued, and moved over to where the voice was coming from. In the corner of the shop was a young woman, with her back towards me, intent on looking at a lovely china doll in a box. Beside her stood a little girl. At first she didn't notice me, but was staring into a beautiful snow globe. As I watched her, unobserved, I was struck by her beauty. She was around four years of age and very petite. It was her hair that particularly fascinated me. It was long, thick, and curly, and the sides were caught up with bright green ribbons. The colour of her hair was a rich, dark auburn.

As I looked at her, she suddenly turned and noticed me. I smiled at her, suddenly aware of the most expressive, huge, green eyes looking back at me. She smiled, cheerily blurting out, 'My sister is a star in heaven. Look!' I was slightly taken aback by the unexpectedness of this remark. Her mother turned to see who it was she was speaking to. I felt slightly embarrassed at this point, but the mother simply smiled at me. In return, I remarked, 'What a delightful little girl.' I could sense the pride in her eyes as she responded, 'Thank you. I think so.'

I turned my attention once again to the little girl who confidently informed me that she had a globe like this at home. She held it up for me to see. The globe was in fact musical, and it played *Twinkle, twinkle little star.* As she held it upside down, the snow fell on a night-time winter scene. Santa and his sleigh flew across the sky, and, above them, just one shooting star could be seen. It was so beautiful, I felt I wanted to watch the scene over and over again.

I asked the little girl her name. 'Anushka,' she replied shyly, holding on to the edge of her Mummy's coat. I looked at her Mum and remarked what a lovely name it was. And so unusual. Her Mum went on to tell me that her great grandparents were Russian, and Anushka was a Russian name.

At this point her little girl was pulling at her skirt. She bent down to see what it was she wanted and was met by a quiet, but insistent little voice. 'Show her the globe. Tell her about Sophie.'

By now, I was intrigued.

Anushka's Mum, without any sense of awkwardness, then disclosed to me that seven years ago her first child had died after only a few days, very suddenly and unexpectedly. Both she and her husband were devastated. Without the Lord, she observed, they couldn't have got through their grief. I felt compelled to ask her if she was a Christian. She beamed a big smile at me and affirmed, 'Yes. Are you?'

Suddenly, there was a sisterly bond between us, and we continued to discuss what had happened at that time. Cathy revealed how God had held their hands when no one else could bring them any comfort. In time, however, they began to see hope for the future again, and she found herself pregnant once more.

Anushka was born on Christmas day. Her sister had died three years before on Christmas Eve.

Cathy told me that a further reason for calling her little girl Anushka was because in Russian it means 'God has favoured us.' When you looked into the eyes of this child, there was no doubt about it.

Anushka announced to me that her sister Sophie was in heaven, like a shooting star. Hence, the significance of the snow globe. Cathy explained that the Lord had, as with Job, taken away from them, on that Christmas Eve. But on Christmas day, three years later, He had given them a new gift. A different one. And she was so grateful.

We so often measure life by years. Yet I remember once reading an observation by Viktor Frankl. 'We cannot judge a biography by its length, or by the number of pages in it. We must judge it by the richness of its content. Sometimes the "unfinished" are among the most beautiful of the symphonies.'

As I walked away from Cathy and Anushka, I realised I was smiling to myself. For, in the midst of busy-ness and crowds, God had reminded me that a life, however short, can touch the hearts of many.

As I went to meet Chris, there was a spring in my step. I couldn't wait to tell him about Anushka. The Lord had also reminded me in a fresh way that this time was about Him. On Christmas day, He had given Cathy Anushka, which was wonderful. Yet, even more amazingly than that, He had given a lost world Jesus. Yes, God had indeed favoured us.

God is so very dear. He prepares and sends people to us, and we wonder why. They cross our paths, and we may never see them again. But their stories live on in our hearts. They reach out to us, and touch us again when we least expect. That's how very much He loves us.

And that's how it was with Anushka. For, at a time not too far distant, when I needed Him to hold my hand, I remembered that sometimes He gives and sometimes He takes away. But we can feel His favour as He blesses our life in inexplicable ways.

It was in the run-up to Christmas that I began to feel unusually tired. Looking back to how I remembered feeling last time I was pregnant, I didn't recall feeling so worn out. Despite being busy over Christmas, I was cosseted by my family and ordered to put my feet up. Nevertheless, as I reflected back on my first pregnancy I was quite sure that on the whole—other than during a few months of sickness at the beginning—I had felt energised and raring to go. Life, whilst not without its challenges, had been pretty wonderful.

We left England just three weeks after our wedding. Our wedding day had been perfect and had been followed by two happy and sunny weeks on the South Coast of England, in a lovely house loaned to us by two dear missionary friends. We then spent another week with my family in Somerset before beginning our new life together, working with the European Christian Mission in La Charité-sur-Loire, in central France.

Life was full, if not a little scary, at times. My French was limited, to say the least. Since no one we knew in the small town spoke English, Chris was my main source of conversation, as well as being my French teacher. As anyone who knows me would appreciate, I love a good chat. That meant, as I so often laughingly declared, at least I couldn't fall out with my new husband, since there was no one else to talk to!

Living in another country had many new and exciting, if

at times daunting, aspects to it. When I became pregnant so
far from home, that was one of those times. Especially with
my still relatively limited French. However, I had no doubts
that we were in the right place. We both had a love for
France and its people which has only continued to grow
over the years.

God had clearly guided us to this place to pioneer a
church-plant. In those earliest days we gathered for worship
in the front room of a French family's home, though in later
years the church, now grown and established, would move
into its own building. Katie's most beloved teddy, called
Arthur, which she still has sitting on her bed, was given to
her by a lady who was one of our first contacts in that town.
But that's another story. And another book.

Life was busy during my pregnancy, supporting Chris in
the church-planting work, studying French—which for me
was a huge challenge in itself, entertaining, and improving
my French culinary skills, on a very limited budget, for our
new French contacts and friends. Life was in fact extremely
busy. Yet, even when heavily pregnant, I had never
experienced the feelings of exhaustion of the past few
weeks of this second pregnancy.

As time went on, I became aware of a feeling of an
unhealthy lethargy that could not be explained.

I quickly reminded myself of the fact that, first time
around, I hadn't already got a lively little handful to look
after. I reflected to myself that all second-time Mums
probably felt the same. Not only that, but this particular little
bundle seemed to be very active indeed, not letting me
forget for one minute that he, or she, had joined the family;
often keeping me awake at night with his, or her, antics.

I smiled to myself as I pondered the question. A
footballer, maybe, or perhaps a ballerina? And my concerns
were quickly allayed.

As time passed, and tiredness remained, I continued to
push any concerns to the back of my mind, thinking to

myself, 'Now, come on. Don't be silly. There's nothing wrong. You're a midwife, for goodness sake. Get a grip.' I felt that I didn't have the excuse that I had used previously, when feeling clueless about some detail, that although I was a midwife, I had never been a mother before. For, now I was a Mum. And the fact is that as both Mum and midwife I was worried.

I talked to the Lord constantly about my worries. They lacked any real concrete foundation, and yet I found no sense of peace. In fact, quite the opposite. A deep sense of foreboding swept over me.

Chris and I discussed at length how I was feeling. His tenderness and caring I shall never forget. He sought to reassure me, time and again.

Yet there was a deep-seated fear that would not leave me.

My midwife insisted there was nothing at all to worry about. The baby was growing and active; the heartbeat was strong and regular. She suggested, kindly, that I was worrying over nothing. Our baby was healthy. In a few weeks, I would be holding it and wondering what all the fuss was about.

I believe that even then God, in His infinite mercy, was preparing me. In a way, I had already begun to grieve for my daughter, without even knowing it.

The 'grief,' although I did not perceive it at the time, was like the experience of going on a glorious mountain walk, captured by the beauty all around, but suddenly becoming aware of discomfort as you feel a tiny stone in your shoe rubbing against your foot. Instead of stopping to remove it, you manoeuvre it into the corner of your shoe and continue on your journey, distracted by the beauty all around you. Then it suddenly wriggles out again, the discomfort of it marring the view before you. Eventually, you are forced to give in, take off the shoe, and remove the stone. It's only once that is done that the pain begins to subside, and you are able to enjoy the scenery once again.

So it is with grief.

It has to be attended to sooner or later.

When, is partly up to us. Scripture tells us that tears will come, but, in the morning, joy. I didn't know it at the time, of course, but the tears and the joy of which God speaks would very soon be ours. As yet, the stone was just beginning to rub and I had no more than a vague awareness that it was there.

It is strange how certain articles, or items, can play a significant part in our lives. For me, it was a lovely wooden rocking chair. Very simple in design, with a bright chintz cushion on its seat, which my Mum had made for it. I had always wanted one. Chris had bought it for me after we were married. I was thrilled, and it had pride of place in our small lounge. We had tried it in various spots in the house, but, because of its particular shape and size, it had to be placed strategically, so that no one fell over it, causing it to be more of an irritation than a pleasure.

When we had finally settled on a spot next to our fireplace, it looked delightful. Every time I came into the room, I found myself glancing across at it with a certain amount of pride. You know how it can be with something new. You almost don't want to use it at first, for fear of spoiling it. But after a time, like anything else, it becomes familiar and you use it, and enjoy it for what it is.

Everyone who came to our little house used to head for that chair—especially the children. It gave hours of comfortable pleasure, and fun. I loved it.

Perhaps that was the reason that on that particular wintery day I found myself sitting in my chair, staring into the firelight. As the chair rocked backwards and forwards, I was aware of the most intense sadness sweeping over me. I guess it caught me unawares, because suddenly, for no reason, I found myself sobbing uncontrollably.

Even as I write, I can still feel the pain. I felt consumed with a grief that I had never known before. As I cried to the

Lord for comfort and understanding, even though the sadness remained, I knew He was there. I remember glancing across at our daily calendar. Through my tears, I read the words from Isaiah 40:11.

'He tends His flock like a shepherd: He gathers the lambs in His arms and carries them close to His heart; He gently leads those that have young.'

Yes, He was with me. I felt like a child again, being scooped lovingly up into my Father's arms. My Dad was my hero, but even he couldn't always save me from sorrow and pain. So I cried to the Lord, 'Abba, Father' (the Aramaic word 'Abba' is, as you may well know, an expression of familiarity that means something like 'Daddy').

He gathered me in His arms, and set me back on my feet. And I knew that whatever the future held, the Great Shepherd of the sheep would lead me to the safety of His fold.

8

STRENGTH TO THE WEARY

As the days passed, I kept busy. I was having all the usual ante-natal checks, and it was during one of these that the midwife noticed that over consecutive weeks I had lost weight quite significantly.

All the fears that I had sought to push to the back of my mind in trying to enjoy the remainder of my pregnancy came galloping back.

I asked to see the obstetrician, which the midwife agreed to arrange at my local hospital. Chris and I prayed together before we left the house for my appointment. We asked that, whatever the outcome, the Lord would help us face it. Both of us were quiet and nervous as we walked hand in hand the length of the hospital corridor, wondering what that outcome might be.

The obstetrician was in fact very reassuring, having performed his examination, and he assured us that everything was going to plan. He had no concerns, as our baby was active, with a strong, steady heartbeat. Its size, though a little on the small side for my expected due date, was perfectly acceptable, especially considering that Katie had weighed only six pounds at birth.

I tentatively asked the consultant whether I could have a scan, as I had been feeling so anxious about my baby for some weeks now, and wanted to reassure both myself and my husband that all was well. In those days, scans were nowhere near as common, or as available, as they are now. They were not the norm, and were generally not contemplated unless there was a suspected problem.

The consultant was insistent that there was absolutely

nothing to indicate the need for a scan, and it wasn't their practice to do one simply to reassure over-anxious parents. As we left the hospital, the feeling of foreboding swept over me again. I longed for someone to listen to me. As I wept in my husband's arms, we convinced ourselves once more that everything was going to be alright.

At thirty-two weeks, I had another ante-natal check.

I was sure I had gained weight, and was feeling more positive. The midwife's look of concern made my heart miss a beat, however. 'You have lost a little more weight, Mrs. Jack. But everything else is looking good.'

On hearing this, I stated in no uncertain terms that I wanted to see the doctor. At this point, I was tired, worried, and weary. She agreed, saying she would make me an appointment. I then became unusually assertive. I declared that I was not leaving the hospital until I had seen a doctor. She could see that I meant business, and sent for the obstetric registrar.

The doctor arrived. Once again he endeavoured to reassure me. I pressed him to allow me to have a scan, however, using my professional status as a lever—something I had never previously done. I was so desperate for support; so convinced that all was not well. I even offered to pay to have a scan.

Finally, the doctor reluctantly complied. I think he had realised by then that if he didn't, he would never get rid of me!

The doctor promised to arrange an appointment for a scan as soon as possible. It had to be booked at the nearest city hospital since our local hospital didn't have the facilities. He advised me to go home and relax. All would be well.

As we left the hospital, I remember remarking to my husband, 'I bet he's glad to see the back of me!' But I really didn't care.

This baby was ours. We loved it.

And we needed to know what was happening with it, and

whether there was anything that needed to be done.

Days passed as I waited impatiently for my appointment to come through. I rang the hospital several times, to no avail. In the end, I convinced myself that I was being the unreasonable one. 'Other people need a scan more than me,' I thought. Perhaps I was being the over-anxious mother. I tried to pray and knew I should be patient. I remember thinking over and over to myself, 'You can do this. You have to be strong.'

I felt terrible. So very weary of it all.

Picking up my Bible, I cried to the Lord again. Through my tears I read these words:

> *Do you not know? Have you not heard? The Lord is the everlasting God, the Creator of the ends of the earth. He will not grow tired or weary, and his understanding no one can fathom. He gives strength to the weary and increases the power of the weak. Even youths grow tired and weary, and young men stumble and fall; but those who hope in the Lord will renew their strength. They will soar on wings like eagles; they will run and not grow weary, they will walk and not be faint.*

(Isaiah 40:28-31)

As I pondered those words of encouragement, I remembered a story shared with me by a dear Christian brother, Duncan, who was an itinerant evangelist.

On one occasion, he was given a lift by an elderly Christian man whose life had been spent in service to the Lord. During the journey, he asked Duncan, 'What is it that you have that God most wants?'

After a few minutes thinking about it, he responded, 'My love?'

'Yes, He wants your love, but that is not it.'

'Err, my commitment?'

'Yes, yes, but what else?'

The conversation continued until finally our evangelist

friend gave up.

'OK! What does He want the most?'

The man stopped the car, looked Duncan straight in the eye, and in his thick, Scottish accent pronounced, 'Why, laddie, He wants your weakness.'

'My weakness?' queried Duncan.

'Aye, laddie. You see, when we are strong in ourselves God cannot use us. But when we realise we are weak, and call upon His strength, it is His power that works through us, not our own. For His strength is made perfect in our weakness.'

Suddenly, I found I was smiling to myself and confessing to Jesus just how weak I was feeling right then. He has broad shoulders, however, and wouldn't let me go.

As I needed His strength, so it would be there.

I only had to ask.

So I did.

What a relief it was, when finally the appointment for my scan came through. I was by this time in my thirty-fifth week. The appointment was for two weeks' time.

Was I disappointed?

Yes!

I wanted it now.

Nevertheless, something within me said, 'Just wait.'

And, finally, peace came.

I don't know why, but I remember feeling like Shadrach, Meshach and Abednego, in Daniel chapter 3. I was about to step into the blazing furnace. Yet I knew, as they did, that the Lord would be beside me, and that when I came out, not a hair of my head would be singed. Moreover, there would not remain even the smell of burning upon me.

In fact, as I took the next step, I was convinced that there would already be a footprint in which to plant my own.

I was almost thirty-eight weeks as I drove, with Chris, the twenty-five miles or so to Bristol Royal Infirmary. The big day had arrived and we were both feeling a little nervous.

But also positive.

I had continued to feel a real sense of God's peace. I simply wanted now to be able to look forward to meeting the new member of our family in, hopefully, just over a week's time.

Chris and I laughed together over my observation that I really did feel and look like a barrage balloon. I had been drinking copious amounts of water before leaving home and on the journey. I wanted to ensure a clear ultra-sound.

As I waddled unceremoniously down the corridor, a new Mum with babe in arms, and with proud Dad in tow, strolled past us. Strange how we remember such incidental things. 'That will soon be us,' I thought to myself. 'Oh, I can hardly wait.'

I remember chatting to a young couple who sat opposite us. The usual questions came up.

Is this your first?

For them it was, and I remember feeling rather proud that this was our second.

Have you agreed on possible names?

We still hadn't decided on a name for a boy or a girl, although we both liked the name Ben, and that was a real possibility if it was a boy.

For some reason, we had struggled to find a girl's name the first time around. Once chosen, we had loved the name Katie. It suited our little girl very well. A second girl's name was proving elusive, however.

It was great chatting to the couple, and it helped the time to pass more quickly. Before too long the wait was over, and it was our turn to be seen.

We were introduced to a pleasant-looking midwife who greeted us with an encouraging smile. She had read our notes, and touched my arm gently. 'I'm sure everything's going to be fine, dear.'

'Thank you,' I replied.

She gave me a gown, informing me that the wait

shouldn't be too long. I certainly hoped not. Not out of impatience, but because of an incredible urge to use the loo (which it was preferable not do to before the scan). Chris teased me in his usual way, and I responded by ordering him not to make me laugh, or he would be on mop and bucket duty.

At last the technician came and led me into a small room. My husband was asked to wait outside, which was commonplace in those days. She suggested to Chris that it would only take five minutes and to have a coffee while he waited. As I looked back at him, he smiled at me reassuringly and at that moment I felt so loved. In my mind, I was playing out the fact that in maybe five or ten minutes I would be hugging him, telling him, 'Everything's OK. Our baby's fine. Let's celebrate. Phone the family, and then have a nice cup of tea. And, yes, a sticky bun.'

As I lay on the bed, making small-talk with the technician, trying hard to normalise the situation, she expertly slid the ultra-sound device across the gel she had put on my, by now, very round belly.

I realised that this was it.

In a few minutes, we would know. And how I would laugh at myself for worrying so.

She first listened to the heartbeat, which boomed out clear and strong. We both smiled, and I thought to myself, 'What a precious sound that is.' I relaxed. I deliberately didn't look at the screen, as I didn't want any hint of the baby's gender. That was for Chris and I to discover together when our baby emerged into the world.

So I watched the technician. As I did, I was aware of a sudden look of concern on her face. 'Is everything all right?' My voice was quiet and unsure. 'Does everything appear normal?' By now, my voice sounded false and shaky, even to my own ears.

'Just give me a minute,' she replied.

That minute was one of the longest of my life.

She laid the scanning device down saying that she would be back in just a moment. 'Mrs. Jack, I need the doctor to come in and check something for me.' She half laughed as she added, 'He's more experienced at ultrasounds than I am.'

Before I could even ask, 'Could you send my husband in?' she was gone. As I lay on the bed, I could hear a clock ticking. Now, as anyone who knows me is aware, I love clocks (especially cuckoo clocks). Yet the constant ticking of this clock was an intrusion on my thoughts.

I suddenly felt very isolated.

Where is she? What's taking so long?

And then, all of a sudden, she was back, accompanied by a young doctor. He introduced himself as a senior registrar. I remember thinking he looked far too young, and wanting him to turn into a wise-looking, older man, who, by his very experience, could make everything alright, and deliver nothing but good news.

Silly, I know, but any straw was worth clutching at.

I asked if my husband could be present. The moment I saw Chris's gentle face, I wanted to protect him, knowing he would be thinking the same about me. That's how it was with us.

But only God himself could protect us. Only He could have prepared us for the words we were to hear next. I now believe that over the previous few months that is exactly what He had been doing, although we didn't fully understand it at the time.

As I clutched at Chris's hand, I remembered Anushka, and her Mum's words to me. 'The Lord held our hand when nobody else could.' This was it, then. This was the reality. We had said on many an occasion that our God made a difference, even in the hardest moments of our lives.

Perhaps, for us, this was to be such a moment.

9

THROUGH THE VALLEY

Amidst the inevitable 'Is there something wrong?' the doctor continued to do the ultrasound. All I could hear was the ticking of the clock, along with the sound of my own heartbeat, which I felt sure everyone in the room could hear.

The doctor turned to look at us, his face strained and anxious. Without any pre-amble, he began telling us how very sorry he was. At that point it felt as though I was watching a scene that I was no longer a part of. I felt frozen in time. And if I could only stop him from uttering one more word, everything would be all right.

I felt Chris's hand tightening around mine, and heard a voice which sounded strangely familiar, and yet nothing like my own, asking, 'What is it, Doctor? What's wrong?' He sat by the bed and very gently informed us that our baby had a life-limiting condition called anencephaly. As a midwife, I knew of this condition, although I had never actually been involved with a Mum whose child had it.

The registrar went on to explain to us both what this meant for our baby: the failure of proper development of the cranium and scalp. The brain, if any, was reduced to small masses. There was also evidence of spina bifida, characterised by defective closure of the bony encasement of the spinal cord.

Yes, yes, so that was the medical terminology, clearly and professionally explained. But what does this mean for our baby?

Is there anything you can do? An operation?

Perhaps you've got it wrong?

Could we have a second opinion?

All these questions, I was fully aware, were futile, and yet I simply had to ask them.

'I'm afraid there is nothing we can do,' he maintained. 'Your baby cannot survive with this medical condition. She may be born alive but could only survive for a few hours at the most.'

'She?' I queried.

'Yes. A little girl.'

So, after all the waiting and wondering, we knew we were having another little girl. A sister for Katie. As I mentioned earlier, we didn't mind what the gender of our baby was—as long as our child was healthy. But now I simply couldn't quite take it in. After dreaming of the moment we would ask, 'Is it a boy or a girl?' for almost nine long months, no one could have prepared us for hearing the answer under these terrible circumstances.

'There has to be something that can be done,' I pleaded. 'This can't be it, surely. There must be another alternative.' As the doctor looked at me, his eyes said it all. He shook his head.

There was, in fact, no hope at all.

The next few hours seemed to pass in a haze of shock, numbness, and disbelief. I felt swept along by this unfolding tragedy. Yet, not swept along in the way I remember experiencing as a child, when, bathing in the sea, a big wave would come along and lift my body effortlessly back onto the safety of the beach, bringing with it a feeling of elation and happiness and the desire for more. This was different altogether. More like a sense of hurtling forwards on my new roller skates, totally out of control. Instead of a warm, soft beach, there would be only the hard ground to land on.

Or, in this case, hard, harsh reality.

We were informed by the registrar that we would be able see the consultant within the next hour or so. He would talk us through the next step. Perhaps we might like to go and have a cup of tea. I smile to myself now, as I remember thinking even then, 'We're on to the inevitable cup of tea routine—as if it were the answer to all that lay ahead.'

And yet, in a strange way, it was a comforting thought. A cup of tea was so very normal. And, with my family, definitely a way of life. As Chris and I wandered hand in hand, in complete silence, into the busy cafeteria, I wondered to myself whether anything would ever feel normal to us again.

Chris found a table in a quieter corner, where I sat while he went to get some tea. There was a small, chipped china vase on the table, and in it one single red rose. The cafeteria itself was rather tatty and gloomy, but served its purpose, I supposed. The table was made of formica, and had definitely seen better days.

Maybe it was because of the dreary surroundings that my eyes settled once again on the simple, yet perfectly formed flower whose richness brightened up the room. As I gently touched its petals, it felt like soft velvet between my shaking fingers. Of course, this flower, for all its perfection, would eventually fade and be gone forever.

Our daughter, on the other hand, despite her tiny body, so seemingly imperfect, had a God-given soul. In the eyes of the Lord, she was perfect.

Although this thought should have brought me some comfort, it didn't. I felt a sudden panic rise within me. Surely this can't be it. All there is. After all the waiting, only death. There has to be a reason. But what? How can any good thing come out of the death of a child?

It was many years later that my question would finally be answered. For the Lord, as He led me through the valley, had many lessons He wanted me to learn.

This was only the beginning.

I remember staring ahead through a window overlooking the car park. People were constantly coming and going, about their business. I became aware of people's idle chatter, and someone laughing in the distance. There was the constant clatter of cups on saucers, of cutlery being cleared from trays. My eyes misted over with unshed tears.

Our baby was going to die.

Yet, seemingly, to the outside world nothing had changed. Didn't they understand that my heart was breaking? Chris came back to the table and set down my cup of tea. I remember stirring it round and round, watching the circles of hot liquid like a whirlpool. I felt trapped, myself, in a whirlpool of grief from which I did not know, at that point, whether I could ever escape.

As promised, within the hour we were sitting opposite a distinguished-looking consultant obstetrician. I asked him to explain further to us the condition anencephaly. He did so, informing us that this was the most serious of a group of abnormalities that come from the embryonic neural tube defects. It was a congenital malformation in which both cerebral hemispheres are absent. He went on to elucidate that although affected infants have intact brainstems, and are able to maintain vital functions, such as temperature regulation and cardiac and respiratory function—sometimes for a few hours, at other times for up to several days—they eventually died of respiratory failure.

The bottom line was that most infants with this condition were in fact stillborn.

I heard myself imploring, 'So there is absolutely no hope, then?' He didn't seem to mind the rather silly question, but simply shook his head, repeating once more how very sorry he was.

He then moved on to the matter in hand: how to manage my labour and the delivery of our daughter. He began to discuss our different options.

As I was almost at full-term, an elective caesarean section was mentioned. The consultant explained that the labour could be long, due to the fact that normally the hard skull of a baby pushed against the cervix to open it, whereas in our baby's case the top of the skull was missing, and therefore labour could be longer, and obviously very traumatic emotionally, granted the inevitable outcome. He left us for a few minutes to give us space to discuss things together.

I remember Chris asking, 'What do you think? Whatever you want is fine with me.' I suddenly wanted to scream at him, 'I don't want any of it. I just want my baby to be whole.' But, as I looked into his pale, anxious face, I realised he was as lost as I was.

We were like two frightened children, needing someone to take control, to tell us everything would be OK.

But we knew it wouldn't.

The hardest thing was that there was no positive option. The ultimate ending would be the same.

There was no one to help us. No one to comfort us.

I felt consumed with fear.

Death was inevitable, and that was that.

I needed some air, so I wandered over to the window. As I opened it, the cold air rushed into my nostrils and took my breath away. I remembered the words, 'He wants your weakness.' But at that moment I felt I had nothing to give—not even that. I felt that I should be angry, yet I wasn't. I was completely overwhelmed by the deepest sadness that I had ever known.

I would love to be able to say that I never asked, 'Why?' That I simply accepted this was God's will for us. However, that would not be honest. 'Why our baby?', 'Why us, Lord?', was going around in my head.

Much later, I came to understand that I need not feel any guilt in those feelings. He didn't mind that I had asked the questions. His love was greater for me than that. For in my weakness and honest questioning there would be, one day, an understanding which at this juncture was far too difficult to grasp.

After discussion, and helpful advice from the consultant, I finally decided to try for a normal delivery. The reason? I simply couldn't bear the thought of being put to sleep and waking up to someone advising me it was all over. It wasn't that I was being terribly brave in facing a labour with the inevitability of a negative end. It was rather that I desperately needed for there to be something in between.

Of course, I knew that physically, emotionally, and spiritually, it was going to be such a challenge.

My mind went back to the day Katie had been born. I recalled the joy that had come flooding into my heart. How excited we had been. Certainly, there had been some apprehension, facing the labour prior to the delivery. Yet, the thought of the joy that was to come soon outweighed any nervousness I had felt. With every painful contraction, it felt like one step closer to seeing our child. His, or her, journey, though long, and to some degree dangerous, would be worth the effort. We would be united as a family, the pain and the hard work quickly forgotten.

Yes, I needed that something in between. Although it is hard to explain why, I simply knew that for me it was right. It gave me time, to be sure, to begin to come to terms with my loss. But, more importantly, perhaps, it gave me the chance to hold on to the child within me for a little while longer.

The doctor accepted our decision and was keen for me to be admitted to the hospital straight away. I was horrified at this suggestion. I needed to go home first to see my little girl. I needed so very much to hold her in my arms and feel her chubby little arms around my neck. I ached to see her.

Had it only been five hours?

It seemed like a lifetime ago.

The consultant agreed to this, but asked me to come back that evening, as he wanted to induce labour as soon as possible.

We then decided to phone my parents and warn them, rather than simply turn up on their doorstep with such bad news. As I dialled their number, I was shaking, and my tummy felt full of butterflies. They answered very quickly, almost as if they had been sitting by the phone— which in their case they probably had—waiting for what they hoped would be good news.

I remember saying to Mum, quite calmly, that the news was very sad. Our baby was really sick and would not survive. We were coming home and would fill them in more fully, then.

Mum simply responded, 'O darling, I'm so sorry. We'll be waiting for you. Dad's here. He sends his love.'

I knew my Dad would be standing at her side, and, as she set the receiver down, they would hold each other and weep for us.

I asked Mum to phone my sister and give her the news. I knew through years of experience that my parents and sister, Sue, would love us and support us through this, the hardest of times. Never pushy. Simply there, as and when we asked. And when we didn't, they would pray.

Even when we couldn't find the energy to do it for ourselves, I knew beyond a doubt they would be lifting us both to the Father. Even as I write these words, the tears fall, and I thank God for the experience of having such a precious sister and loving parents in my life.

It was a lonely journey home.

On the way to the hospital we had still held out hope that all my concerns had been misplaced. Now they were a reality, and we faced an uncertain few days.

The sun was shining, which somehow felt completely out of place to me. We tried to make small-talk but gave up in the end.

The silence hung over us like an unwelcome cloud.

As we walked up to my parents' cottage, Dad had been watching for us and opened the door before we even reached it. He smiled reassuringly and hugged me as I walked past him through the porch. He patted Chris warmly on the shoulder. No one knew what to say. It was awkward.

Dad is such a gentle man, full of compassion, yet was at a

loss for words. 'I'll put the kettle on. Here's your Mum.' Mum was coming down the stairs with Katie. 'Look who's here,' she said. Our eyes met across the room. Here was my Mum. She didn't need to say anything. Her eyes said it all.

Katie grinned at us both, her huge, blue eyes shining, her brown curls bobbing. I picked her up and felt I would never be able to let her go. She simply wriggled, and giggled, and squealed 'Mummy, too tight, too tight.' She was so very perfect. So beautiful. And I was grateful to God for her. 'But why did her sister have to be so damaged?' I asked myself.

No answer came, until much, much later.

Leaving Katie to sleep over with my parents, I went home to pick up the neatly-packed bag that had been ready for weeks now. I had felt so confident packing it this time. I knew what to expect.

'How wrong can you be?' I thought, as I grabbed some things from the bathroom before heading for the car.

I didn't look back. I just wanted to go. No point in hanging around. As I passed the newly-decorated nursery, my hand rested briefly on the door knob. No. Do that later, not now. It will be too hard. Without a second glance, I was sitting next to Chris in the car. He looked across at me. I stared ahead thinking, 'Just don't look at the love and concern in his eyes, and then you will cope.'

Chris started the engine and we were off on the most difficult journey we had ever taken together. I felt his hand reach over and touch mine, and was aware of tears silently sliding down my cheeks. 'I'm here,' he tenderly reassured me. I looked at him and felt his pain.

Although I could not find the words to speak to the Lord at that point, I was aware that He was speaking to me, through the familiar words of Psalm 23. 'Even though I walk through the valley of the shadow of death, I will fear no evil for you are with me; your rod and your staff, they comfort me.' (v.4).

10

BEST-LAID PLANS

When Chris and I were in Israel some years ago, we had the joy of visiting a centre run by Messianic Jews. It was a wonderful experience, and we learned much about the way of life in biblical times as we eagerly soaked up more and more about the faith and culture of the people.

I remember our guide explaining to us how olive oil was made: how the olive stone had to be completely crushed to extract the oil. I was reminded of that when we visited France recently. We were in an area where we were surrounded by beautiful vineyards which looked wonderful as they basked in the warmth of the sunshine. There the vines sat, row after row, with heavy bunches of lush red grapes hanging from them, waiting to be picked at grape-harvest—the vendange—in September.

Now it's true that both olives and grapes are delicious simply picked and eaten. Nevertheless, to extract the precious oil and juices needed to make olive oil and wine, the olives or grapes need to be completely crushed, in order to make the most of all that their fruit has to offer.

Sometimes, in life, we may find ourselves almost crushed by our circumstances. We feel we cannot understand what is going on.

Can there be any point to our suffering?

Can a loving God be part of all this?

Like the olives and the grapes, however, and just as the beautiful petals of flowers are crushed to release their scent, to make oil for perfume that many can appreciate and share the benefit of, so God at times chooses to use our suffering to release His power to touch the lives of those around us.

Yet so often in life it is only in hindsight that we see the meaning behind God's plan for us.

The Bible reminds us that we walk by faith, not by sight (2 Cor 5:7). That means a whole heap of trusting has to be done at such times.

Easy? No.

Possible? Yes.

The reason? No one has ever given up as much for His children as our Heavenly Father. In Isaiah, we read that He goes through the fire and through the flood with us (Is 43:2). Of course, He will never force Himself on us. It is always our choice whether to trust Him or not.

Looking back again to our time in Oberammergau, I am reminded of our visit to one of the little carpenter's shops in the village. This particular carpenter had played the part of Peter in the Passion Play. It seemed strange to see him now, going about his every-day job.

As we watched him work, he took up a block of rough wood and quickly and adeptly began to carve small pieces out of it. At first, you couldn't see what it was he was fashioning. And then, before our eyes, it became clear: the rough wooden block had become the most beautifully crafted hand of Christ. Tucked inside the hand was the figure of a child.

As I looked at it, the hand was perfection in its structure. As its fingers gently curled around the little girl, the back of the hand showed soft gentle curves, holding the child so gently, as if she might break.

There was also a similar carving on the old bench the carpenter worked on. I picked it up, expecting the same model. But this hand was different. It held a little boy. Once again, the fingers gently curled around the child, but the back of the hand showed the muscles and sinews to be harder, more prominent: those of a father protecting his son.

The carvings were quite unique and immediately spoke to

me of the Father's love for us.

On the wall at home I have a beautiful pencil-sketch done for me by a friend. It is of a father holding in his arms his son. It is the prodigal. The picture is of a father's love, his arms strong and powerful. You can see the taught muscles of his arms as they hold on to his son, who was lost and has returned to him. And yet there is also such a tenderness about the way he holds him.

Chris kindly bought me the lovely carvings. Yes, both of them. Whenever I look at them, I am reminded that I am held, whatever my circumstances.

And when my arms are not holding on to Him, He still holds on to me.

I recently came across a book by John Ortberg with a fascinating title. *If You Want to Walk on Water, You've Got to Get out of the Boat.* What a true picture of faith that is.

Scary?

Yes, perhaps it is.

But only if you get out of the boat on your own.

So here I was, getting out of the boat. Would I walk or sink? That was the question I asked myself as we drove towards the hospital.

It was around six o'clock, and already dark. How I longed for light and sunshine. Everything seemed so much gloomier when the nights drew in so early, and I wondered how many more moments in my life there might be like this one.

I felt I was being forced out of the boat.

I didn't have a choice, as Peter did. And yet, in an important way I did. For I could choose to look down at the swirling dark water that would sweep me away, or look up and grab hold of the hand that reached down to me. The hand of a carpenter, rough and gnarled, hardened by its labours. But also the hand of the Crucified One.

For there it was. The hole where the nail had pierced His hand—the scarred hand that speaks of sacrifice. I knew that if I could find the courage to hold on to that hand now, I would not sink, but walk.

Despite all I knew, still at times I found it so very hard.

So where does the strength come from? Jesus alone.

Around twenty minutes into our journey, about half-way to the hospital, our old car began to make very strange noises. Chris suggested that we had better stop at the next garage. All I could think was, 'O Lord, surely we're not going to break down. Not tonight, of all nights.'

As we drove into the garage, it was clear that all was not well with our car. As we went inside, the woman at the small reception desk greeted us warmly. 'Can I help you?' she enquired, in her strong west country accent. 'I'm not sure,' Chris responded. 'I think there's a problem with our car. Is there someone who could have a look at it for us?'

We were feeling less than hopeful, as the woman seemed to be the only one around. 'We are on our way to the hospital,' Chris added, hoping this might help our cause. 'Oh, I see.' She smiled, looking at my round tummy. 'Let me see what I can do.' Chris's comment had obviously had the desired effect.

After a while, a young man came and asked what the problem seemed to be. He and Chris went outside and I sat, feeling like a beached whale, in the reception area. I was fully aware that the woman kept looking at me. That wasn't surprising, really, as my large frame, spread across the less-than-comfortable tiny wooden chair, must have looked quite comical to her as she constantly glanced across in my direction.

Unusually for me, I wasn't in the mood for a chat. So I kept my eyes focused on my, by now, rather chubby feet.

After half an hour or so, I felt rather churlish not making any effort to speak to the woman. I asked her if it would be possible to have a glass of water. Her response was immediate. 'Of course you can, my lovely. I nearly asked you before, but you seemed deep in thought, and I didn't want to bother you. Thought you might be in early labour, or something.'

Without waiting for a response from me, she was off, and was soon back with my water. 'What a time for your car to break down.'

'Yes,' I agreed.

'You must be ever so excited. Are you on your way to the hospital to have your baby?'

Before I could respond, she was off again.

'Oh, I think its wonderful. What do you want? A boy or a girl? But then you probably don't mind, so long as it's healthy. At least, that's what everyone says, isn't it?'

She then entertained me with stories of different relatives who had had babies very quickly, some not even getting to the hospital in time.

'Still,' she offered, 'you wouldn't want to have your baby in a garage, would you?'

I felt at this point she was trying to reassure herself, rather than me.

'Don't worry,' I managed to respond, 'I'm not in labour yet.'

'Oh, that's all right, then.' She smiled with relief.

After providing me with more water, she set off again, 'Anyway, as I was telling you . . .'

And so she continued to regale me with her stories, even making me laugh at some of her expressive turns of phrase, and at her stories, which were embellished for good effect. Of that I was certain.

As I saw Chris and the mechanic walking towards the garage, I realised that over an hour and a half had gone by. As I listened to the lady, I found myself smiling, and thanking God for her. She had kept me occupied with her funny stories. Yet, surprisingly, she had not once pressed me for any information about myself. How wise the Lord is! He sometimes uses the most unexpected of people to support us on our journeys.

If our car had to break down—and that's just life, isn't it?

—what better place for it to happen than this? The Lord not only provided a mechanic, but also a wonderfully down-to-earth, kindly lady to support me in ways she would never know.

Chris informed me that the car was fixed. However, before leaving the garage, we decided to phone the hospital to explain our delay. The ward sister suggested that due to the lateness of the hour it would now make more sense for me to go back home and return at eight o' clock the following morning.

So, after calling my parents to let them know, we began our journey home.

'Bye, my lovely,' the kindly lady called out, as we left.

'Thanks for everything,' I replied as I walked towards the car.

'Oh, my lovely, I didn't do anything.'

'You will never know how much you did,' I thought to myself as we drove away.

It had been a long day for us. And one thing was certain. Nothing had gone to plan.

No plan of ours, anyway.

Suddenly, I was lost in my thoughts. Before I knew it, we were nearly home again.

As we drove through our little village, I noticed many lights on in the different houses. Just for a moment, I wondered about the lives of the people who lived there. What had their day been like? What did tomorrow hold for them?

Chris got out of the car and came round to open the door for me. As I got out, for the first time that I could ever remember, I felt afraid to go into my own home. It was as if going through the door would set in motion a negative chain of events that no one could stop.

As we entered, it felt cold and empty.

It was not because the heating was off, or the lights didn't work. It was rather because I entered with the sure knowledge that I would never now walk through my front door with our tiny baby daughter. She was never coming home.

Tomorrow she would be born.

And tomorrow she would likely die.

11

CARROW PODS AND TEAR JARS

As I looked out through our bedroom window at the clear frosty night, the sky was full of stars. Usually for me a sign of hope that God was in His Heaven, in control, and that all was well with the world, it felt at that moment that all hope had gone.

I knew that this night would be one of the saddest and loneliest of my life so far. I could see His handiwork all around, and yet could draw no comfort from it.

I could see His creation.

Yet, at that moment in time, I seemed to have lost sight of the Creator.

Chris and I hardly spoke as we got ready for bed. As we lay there, we seemed unable to comfort one another, lost in our own thoughts, our own grief. I tossed and turned, trying to get comfortable. On the one hand, I wanted to sleep, so that I didn't have to think any more. On the other hand, I wanted to stay awake, knowing that, as long as the morning didn't arrive, our daughter was still safe and secure inside me.

I went over and over in my head what had happened during the day; perhaps, in some crazy way, hoping for a different ending.

I dreaded the morning.

As I lay there, I was aware that my baby was becoming more and more active. At any previous time, that activity would have been so very welcome. To feel our child moving within me. Such a joy. However, I could now hardly bear it.

I tried getting out of bed, walking around in an attempt to calm her activity. I remember thinking, 'Please stop moving. You are going to die, so what's the point?', only for this to be followed by the awful sense of guilt that swept over me as my own words accused me of being selfish and an unloving mother.

In the next moment, I was weeping, and wanting with all of my heart to feel her. To rest my hand on her little foot as it pushed its way where it could be felt on my tummy, knowing that this time was all I would have with her.

Tomorrow there would be no more activity.

Our baby would be still forever.

How could I find the courage to do this? 'I can't go through with it,' I thought. But I knew that I must. I had no choice. Our baby girl had to be born.

I recalled, then, the agony that Jesus went through before His arrest and crucifixion. I was reminded how He had called to his Father in such anguish that He sweat drops of blood. He asked His Father, if it were possible, to let this cup pass from Him, so that He would not have to suffer the agonies of the cross. Yet He prayed, 'Not my will, but yours be done.'

I knew that He understood my pain, and that He would get me through this. All I wanted now was to sleep. To find some peace before I had to face the morning.

Finally, the night was over. As the day dawned, bright, frosty, and sunny, we set off for the hospital. When we passed the garage we had visited the night before, I looked to see if the lady was there, remembering her kindness to me.

At that point, I felt quite calm. It wasn't until we were close to the hospital that I began to feel more and more anxious and afraid: butterflies in my tummy, and a feeling of nausea and light-headedness. I kept talking to myself, in my head, trying to stay calm. 'Don't be so ridiculous. You are just feeling anxious. Get a grip!'

So, where was God? In those moments I felt no sense of His presence with me.

I have since learnt the important lesson that faith is not in feelings, but in trusting. Sometimes we are hurting too much, or we are in too deep a state of shock, because of our particular circumstances, to feel that God is with us. The simple fact is this: He is always present. Of that there is no doubt.

More recently, while reading the book *The Shack*, I came to appreciate that when Jesus cried to the Father, 'My God, My God, why have you forsaken me?', He hadn't been forsaken at all. He had *felt* forsaken, for sure. That represented the reality of his feelings.

But it was not reality.

God has promised, in His Word, that He will never leave us or forsake us (e.g. Deut 31:6). I thank God that this is the case. That this is reality. For, if we had to rely merely on the roller-coaster of feelings and emotions that we experience in life, we would have no security at all.

So often our attitudes and actions are based on the emotions of the time. God's are not. They are constant and faithful. In His unconditional love, and the promise of his presence, we can fully trust.

After arriving at the hospital, the midwife helped me to settle in. I was put into a side-room. The midwife was kind and attentive, explaining everything to me as she went. My labour would be induced, and she was sorry for the circumstances in which we found ourselves. Within the hour, the doctor had examined me, broken my waters, and set up an intravenous infusion that would start my contractions.

It wasn't long before I experienced the gentle tightening around my tummy. This was familiar ground. It sent my thoughts hurtling back to the day I was woken up in labour. The day that Katie was born. I remembered feeling so different then. Anxious, yes, but very excited at what was to come.

Now it was so very different, and I was filled with such a dread. Everything in me wanted to get off the bed, and run away. It was not the thought of the physical pain. I knew that I could handle that. I had done it before with Katie. No, it was the fact that then I believed the pain was worth it, because it would, God willing, produce a beautiful baby of our very own. That's what gets you through labour pains. That wonderful prospect.

This was different. I felt my heart was breaking.

All this pain, and then . . . nothing.

Only death.

And the most powerful sense of disappointment imaginable.

Labour was long and hard.

After six hours, I had had enough of gas and air and needed pethidine. I remember feeling such a sense of tiredness and isolation, as though I was carrying this completely on my own. Strangely enough, it was the emotional pain that was so hard to bear.

Chris prayed with me at various times, which was wonderful, as I had no energy to pray for myself. I knew that my parents were holding a prayer meeting in their home that evening. Just knowing that made such a powerful difference to me. Friends from our church, where Chris was the minister, would be gathered there, thinking of us, loving us.

There is such a joy in being part of the Christian family, with all its ups and downs at times. Christians make mistakes. We sometimes get it wrong, because God hasn't finished His work in any of us, yet. To know, however, that these dear ones were part of this journey, feeling this pain with us, gave me a profound sense of humility and comfort. I couldn't help but feel held.

As the hours went by—fourteen in all—I was transferred to the large, airy labour ward. By this time, I was becoming more and more distressed with each contraction. The doctor decided to give me an epidural injection in my spine to help me with the pain. Over the next hour or two this had some positive effect.

Sixteen hours had now passed, and I began to feel very sick and dizzy. Suddenly, I felt as though I had no control, and that I was drifting into an abyss. It was the first time that I had actually felt frightened for myself. Something was very wrong. Little did I know that the entourage of doctors and midwives now in attendance had become increasingly concerned about my condition.

I began to haemorrhage badly.

I heard the doctors murmuring that if I hadn't delivered in half an hour they would give me a caesarean section. I knew enough to be aware that at this stage it was now about my safety, and not the baby's. For her, there was no further hope.

I knew within my heart that she was already gone.

Our little girl would be stillborn.

Chris was there the whole time, holding my hand, mopping my brow, talking to me, giving me sips of iced water, and sometimes even managing to make me smile. I knew that he was praying constantly. As the labour dragged on, his mounting fear, I learned later, was that he might also lose me that night.

It is easy to forget how hard it is for a father at such a time. Especially in such difficult circumstances. Since that time, I have had many dads share with me their own heartbreak at the loss of their child. It has humbled me to listen to their stories and personal heartache. And it has given me a deeper understanding of what such a loss means to them.

I felt my body giving up.

Chris was by my side, his face as white as a sheet, fear in his eyes.

I had no strength left.

I knew an operation was now probably inevitable, but the thought of being put to sleep at this stage filled me with fear.

I looked at the time. It was five fifty a.m. I felt the bleeding becoming worse, my strength leaving me. I knew that I was minutes from going to theatre.

My life was in danger.

Suddenly, from out of nowhere, the words from Psalm 46 came to my mind.

> *'God is our refuge and strength, an ever-present help in trouble. Therefore we will not fear, though the earth give way and the mountains fall into the heart of the sea. . . . "Be still and know that I am God."'*

God is my strength. Suddenly, I knew that I could do this.

I began to push with a renewed strength that I know was from God alone. As each pain shot through my body, I cried out to the Lord, and screamed for it to be over.

In just five minutes, it was.

At six a.m. our daughter was born.

She did not breathe.

She was already gone from us—forever.

The timing was perfect, as it always is with God. But I will explain that to you later.

I entitled this chapter 'Carrow Pods and Tear Jars.' Those words are drawn from recollections of things I learned on a trip to Israel.

Whilst there, we visited Yad Vashem, the holocaust museum and memorial near Jerusalem. Within the vast expanse of this unique and moving place is found the Avenue of the Righteous. The Avenue of the Righteous Among the Nations—to give it its full title—is a place where trees have been planted in remembrance of special individuals, non-Jews, who acted nobly towards Jews, often at great cost to themselves, during the time of the

Holocaust.

One such person was Oscar Schindler—the subject of Steven Spielberg's hauntingly powerful film *Schindler's List*—who was responsible for saving thousands of lives from the Nazi death camps.

As we walked through the garden, I asked our guide what the trees were that lined the avenue. She explained to me that they are carrow trees, and that the pods which hang from them contain seeds which can be eaten, and which taste like chocolate. This was a fact that went down very well with me, being something of a chocoholic myself! She then went on to explain that if a carrow tree is burned to the ground, it will, in time, rise up and grow again from the ashes, and how the Israelis see in this an analogy of Israel herself. Destroyed so many times by wars, she has yet risen again and again to become great and powerful.

This takes me back once more to the story of Job. After hearing that he had lost everything, he was nevertheless able to assert, 'Naked I came from my mother's womb, and naked I shall depart. The Lord gave and the Lord has taken away; may the name of the Lord be praised.' (Job 1:21). He was all but destroyed by his circumstances, yet, just like the carrow tree, he would rise again.

If God could raise him up, He can do the same for us.

There is a gift shop in the Avenue of the Righteous where I bought a small earthenware jar. It is a tear jar. It was explained to me that the name derives from the fact that, in earlier times, after the death of a loved one, the women would weep and collect their tears in the jars as part of their grieving. It occurred to me that many a baby and child would have died in those days, and many tears would have been shed and collected.

I knew for certain that however strong my faith, and God's certain support and comfort to me, were, there would be many tears shed for the loss of our tiny baby girl.

But that was alright.

The Lord had given, and He had taken away.

Although, at this point in time, I couldn't in all honesty thank God for that, I did believe that one day all would become clear and that, after the tears, there would once again be joy.

From start to finish, I was in labour for almost twenty hours. I was exhausted in every possible way. Having lost a lot of blood, I was very weak, and I found it hard to function in any coherent way. I was aware of the midwife cutting the umbilical cord, separating my baby from myself. She quickly and quietly wrapped her in a sheet.

Within what seemed no time at all she had whisked her out of the room.

How did I feel?

On the one hand, a sense of relief that the pain was gone. On the other hand, utter and total disbelief. And an overwhelming sense of isolation, the like of which I had never before, nor have I since, experienced.

The next moment, a very young midwife, whom I did not know, was at my side, explaining that she had come on duty for the day shift, and would be taking over from the night staff. She looked about fifteen—a sure sign that I was getting older!

She nervously asked me if I wanted to see the baby.

I remember staring at her and thinking, 'What is she talking about? Where is my baby?'

I hadn't realised that I had actually uttered the words. I thought that they were simply in my head.

The midwife informed me that she had been taken away.

'It's normal practice in the case of a stillborn child. So, do you want to see her?'

I recalled my friend Carol's words to us. 'Look at her, if you can. Seeing her then will help you later.'

I asked the midwife what to her ears must have seemed a rather stupid question. 'What does she look like?'

It was a plea, really.

A cry from the heart.

Tell me that she looks normal. That she is beautiful. So that I will not be afraid, and be able to look at her.

I remember her words, and the look on her face, as if it were yesterday. Her expression said, Why was I asking such questions? What difference did it make now? What she actually verbalised was that she had severe abnormalities of the head and top part of her face, as you would expect, and had spina bifida.

I remember looking at her for some words of comfort, or encouragement. She just stared back at me, clearly not knowing quite what to say next.

It was not her fault. She was young and inexperienced. Perhaps dealing with her first stillborn baby. Had it been either of my dear friends, Carol, or Rose, both of whom were experienced midwives, I know that they would have sat with me, and given me time to make such a decision with Chris. They would have understood the need for some space after what had been such a traumatic birth and negative ending.

What this young woman did not appear able to grasp was that for nine months I had imagined my baby looking as perfect as our first-born. Now, all of a sudden, I was desperately afraid that what I would see would remain in my mind for ever.

I turned to Chris, who was also exhausted, and asked him what he wanted to do. He smiled at me, held my hand, and replied that whatever I wanted was fine with him.

Even as I mouthed the words, 'I think it would be easier not to see her,' somewhere deep within me stirred an unease that perhaps at some point I would bitterly regret the decision made that day, and wonder, 'Why didn't the midwife ask me again? Why didn't she give us another opportunity?'

Of course, as I have already indicated, it was no one's fault. In those days, unlike now, it wasn't the norm to hold your dead child, to have a photo of her, or him, to treasure —a lock of hair, or a tiny hand and footprint of your baby to take away, to hold within your heart.

For us, the opportunity to store those precious memories away would be lost forever.

It was only years later, through my experience of working at a Children's Hospice, that I really came to understand the value of these things. How I thank God, though, that things have now changed, and that greater experience and awareness has brought about a deeper understanding of how to support those who are grieving. Not least by encouraging them to express that grief in all its varied and individual aspects.

What a difference that would have made to Chris and me at that time in our lives.

Yet, had things been different then, there are many lessons that we have learned along the way that would not have been learned. And in consequence, other people whose lives have been touched since through our experiences then would not have been helped as they have been. And this book would in all likelihood not have been written.

As I had lost so much blood, I needed several blood transfusions. I also had a tear in my cervix, which had to be sown up. When I was practising as a midwife and such a job had to be done, either due to a tear, or, on occasion, because a mum had to have an episiotomy to get her baby out more quickly, I would chat away with her about her little one who was either in the crib, or being held by a happy daddy.

But I was aware that in the room where I was there was nothing.

No happy chatter. No smiles or laughter.

Just a job being professionally completed.

And an awkward silence.

I was then given a wash, and the young midwife kindly asked me if I wanted a cup of tea, or something to eat. It all sounded so normal, once again. This time, however, there would be no crying baby to rush down to the nursery to see. No long-suffering midwife, as with Katie, to reassure me that my baby was asleep.

In fact, there was nothing.

Only the sound of a spoon being stirred in a cup. And then . . . silence.

Most of that day I slept, after insisting that Chris go home to see Katie and catch up on some sleep. I knew he would be well looked after by my parents.

It was hard letting him go, even for a few hours. He had been my constant support and rock throughout my ordeal. When the door closed behind him, I felt vulnerable again. Nevertheless, exhausted, I slept.

I only woke on hearing someone enter the room. As I looked around, it was the first time I was really aware of my surroundings. I realised that I had been wheeled from the labour room and put into a side room. I must have dozed on and off while waiting for Chris to return.

On opening my eyes, I realised that it was the midwife who had come into the room, carrying a small glass vase with three red roses in it. 'One of the Mums left these and I thought you might like them to brighten your room,' she commented, smiling broadly at me.

What a lot had happened since the last time I had sat staring at the single red rose in the dingy cafeteria.

Was that really only two days ago?

It seemed so much longer.

Suddenly, everything came flooding back. Yet, instead of feeling sad and full of the sort of emotions I would have expected, I felt nothing. Nothing, that is, other than the most intense feeling of loneliness.

Still feeling exhausted, I put my hand down onto my tummy—something that had become second nature over the past months. As I did so, anxiety filled me from head to toe. My tummy felt soft, and empty, and wobbly.

'She is gone,' I thought. 'My baby is gone.'

There was only emptiness now. I quickly took my hand away, for it only reminded me of my empty womb. And that only served to heighten my sense of failure in not giving birth to a healthy child.

Everyone was kind, but no one really knew what to say to me. The little health care assistant kept popping in to straighten my blanket, and plump up my pillows. Bless her. She was very kind, and I knew that by these simple acts she was trying to comfort me.

Yet, for some reason—I couldn't understand why—it irritated, rather than helped.

Why doesn't anyone talk to me about what has happened? Anything, rather than this sense of everyone seemingly ignoring me, and all that had gone on only a few hours ago.

Why wasn't I crying, or feeling anything?

What was wrong with me? 'Lord,' I prayed, 'let me feel again.

Even if it hurts.

Anything will be better than this dreadful sense of nothingness.'

A short while later, there was a knock on my door and an older lady looked around the door. I invited her to enter. With a big smile on her face, she chirped in a broad Bristol accent 'Hello, my dear. I'm the cleaner. I've just popped in to empty your bin.'

'That's fine. Go ahead,' I responded.

After she had completed her task, she came over to the bed, still smiling, and enquired, 'Where's your lovely baby then? What did you have, a boy or a girl?'

As I write these words, I can still feel the strange sensation in the pit of my stomach as I replied, 'A little girl.' I didn't want to say more, so as not to embarrass her. However, she continued with her questions.

'How lovely. What's her name?'

'We haven't settled on a name yet.'

'Oh, well, perhaps I'll see her later. Is she in the nursery?'

'Actually, I'm not sure where she is. She died, you see.'

The poor lady's eyes filled with tears as she said how sorry she was. That she didn't know. Nobody had told her.

'Please don't worry,' I reassured her.

As she walked out of the door, she looked back at me, apologising, 'If I had known, I wouldn't have said anything.'

And then she left. I felt so sorry for her. I could see that she felt so awkward and upset. 'Is that how it was going to be, then?' I thought, struck by the realisation that this sadness did not only touch our lives, but many others.

Yes, our Heavenly Father really does work in mysterious ways, and uses all kinds of situations and people to touch our lives.

He had in fact answered my prayer to feel again.

Because, for the first time, I had acknowledged to someone—in this case a complete stranger—that my daughter was no more.

This strangely released me from the grip of the fear, so very real at the time, of admitting to myself that she was dead. Thus, for the first time, and most certainly not the last, I might add, the floodgates opened. I began to sob as if I would never stop.

I had asked God to let me feel again, even if it hurt. He answered my prayer, but I was not prepared for the even deeper hurt that was to come.

In fact, during the next six years, I could have filled the tear jar many times over.

12

Perfect Timing, Elsie

The following morning, the consultant came to see me. I enquired what was going to happen to our baby. No one had spoken to us about her since her birth.

What was the next step?

The consultant undertook to ensure someone came to see us about any arrangements we wished to make. He added that if I felt up to it I could be discharged after the weekend.

It was now Friday.

I pointed out that I really didn't want to stay in hospital. For one thing, from my room I could hear the other babies crying, which made it so much harder for me. I also felt fine physically. Just very tired. I added that this was a really special weekend in the life of our church. 'My husband is the minister,' I persisted, 'and we are having our first church weekend away.' I threw in that my friend, who was a midwife, would be there. This latter point seemed to help put his mind at rest regarding me going home so soon after such a traumatic birth.

I informed, almost pleaded with, the consultant that, if possible, I would like to go home that day, and then go away to Devon the following day. I knew that most of the church would be going to Brunel Manor, the conference centre in Torquay that we were using, that evening. After a night in our own home, if all was well, we could then join them on the Saturday.

Naturally, the church weren't expecting Chris still to go and lead the weekend after all that had happened. Nevertheless, for some crazy reason, considering all that we had been through, I knew that it was the right thing to do.

When Chris arrived, I gave him the news that the consultant had agreed that if I really felt up to going home, I could. Only if I really felt strong enough, however, should I go away for the weekend.

Chris was very concerned.

He wanted, as always, to put my best interests first. I stressed that this really felt right to me. I could rest there as well as at home. Furthermore, people that we loved, and that loved us, would surround us both. Whether or not he was entirely convinced, he concurred. It was decided that this was what we would do.

My parents, my sister, her husband Les, and their three children were all due to travel down to Brunel Manor that evening. Although none of them really wanted to go, I encouraged them that this felt right for us all. I promised them that if I didn't feel up to it the following day, Chris and I would stay at home.

Chris spoke with one of my dearest friends, Carol—the midwife I mentioned earlier—who, in God's providence, was also joining us for the weekend away. She agreed to come to our house first, to be there when we got home in the evening. She would then either go on to Brunel that evening, or accompany us the following day. Having such a friend around for us at that time was a real comfort to us both.

All the arrangements were made, except one.

While Chris and I were chatting, a man knocked the door and entered the room. He was an older man, with a kind, grandfatherly face. He introduced himself as one of the hospital chaplains. He had come to discuss any arrangements for our baby.

Suddenly, my heart was pounding. For a little while I had been taken up with thoughts of home and seeing some of the people I loved most, blotting out in my mind the reason for my being in hospital in the first place.

I dislike the phrase 'in denial,' but, yes, denial had slipped in without my even noticing.

Now, I had to face the heartache once again.

Here was this stranger standing before us, wanting us to make arrangements for our dead child. I was struck afresh with the thought, 'Can this really be happening to us?' Coupled with that thought came the all-too-real anxiety and fear that I would not be strong enough to face this.

The Chaplain was very kind, and gentle, as he conveyed to us how sorry he was for our loss. He went on to explain that, in such cases as these, it was normal practice for the baby to be laid in a little white coffin, with a blessing offered by him, as Chaplain. The child would then be buried in a quiet, consecrated area in the hospital grounds.

He assured us that everything would be done with the greatest care and dignity. He concluded with the reassurance that, in their experience, this procedure saved any added grief to the parents and family of the child at such a distressing time.

I remember looking at Chris, and responding, 'Yes, well, if that's what you usually do, that's probably the best thing.'

Chris indicated his agreement.

Of course, at that point in time neither of us really knew what the best thing was. How could we? We were still in shock. Our daughter was dead, and we were still trying to come to terms with the fact that it had happened to us.

Since the Chaplain was so very tender and understanding as he spoke to us, and as no alternative was offered, we both felt that to give our child into his safe hands seemed the right thing to do.

As Christians, we believed firmly that the soul of our baby girl was with Jesus.

She was safe.

Her little body, although born with such deformities, was now made perfect through Him. The same God who reminds us that not a sparrow falls to the ground without His knowledge reminded me that she was now safe and in

His care. She had gone to a far better place where we all long one day to be.

She was free from her infirmities.

Not just happy, but blessed.

I realised that up to that point I had been thinking about all that she would miss in this life, when the real truth was that one day in heaven would be better than a thousand on this earth. We would miss her. But she would miss nothing. Knowing this gave me a new sense of comfort.

The fact that a gentle stranger would be with her on the final stage of her brief earthly journey was therefore alright, because the real journey to heaven had already been made. And she hadn't needed us for that. For only God can give the gift of eternal life.

Our little daughter was now safe.

And that was all that mattered, wasn't it?

In our ignorance, and also, I guess, our innocence, we were to find out only later that although the beliefs and faith behind these reflections hold true, to grieve is also a gift from God.

It was, in fact, some years later, when I felt that my heart would break over the regrets of all that happened over those two days—regrets that touched me as a mother so very deeply—that I learned that it is never too late to grieve. Never too late to find that peace that Jesus speaks of which passes all our understanding.

So it was, later that day, that I gathered my belongings in readiness for going home.

It should all have been so different; felt so different.

Chris would have been holding my bags and bits and pieces, grinning from ear to ear. And I would have been holding our beautiful baby girl, overjoyed with the prospect of taking her home and sharing her with her sister and those within our world.

Instead, there was just a small case.

Nothing else. Just that.

As I turned back and looked one last time into the room that had been my sanctuary, I whispered goodbye to my baby for what I thought then—though it was not the case—the last time.

Once again, my eye caught sight of the bright red roses, with their soft petals. I remembered the rose in the cafeteria. At that time, even as I had admired its beauty, somehow all I could think about was that it would soon fade and die.

But this felt so different, somehow. It was as if it were a glimpse of beauty at a time of despair: a feeling of hope. Although, if I am honest, at that moment I was too heartbroken to see it, I have since been reminded that our hope is in God, who can rescue us from our deepest despair.

I came to understand that it doesn't happen overnight. Yet, if we trust Him, it will happen. When our heart is broken, He will take it, piece by piece, and put it back together again.

When we arrived home, Carol was there to greet us. My parents had taken Katie down to Brunel Manor with them. They would bring her back to us if we weren't able to go the following day. I couldn't wait to see her. But we knew this space was important, to allow us to sort out our own emotions first.

I smile to myself, now.

Sort out our own emotions.

If only it could be that easy.

Carol had made a meal for us. She is an excellent cook, but wasn't used to my cooker. I remember the sausages being rather well done. For the first time over the past few days, it made us laugh. She was such a good sport about it. She insisted she had done it on purpose, really, to give us something to smile about. Strange how, even now, I can remember that moment as if it were yesterday. Most of all, it reminds me of her loving kindness to us at that time.

Despite the fact that we were exhausted, and emotionally drained, we chatted a lot that evening.

It was as if we were trying to shut out the silence.

For, had our newborn babe been there, it would have all been so different: Katie, so full of chatter and excitement because her new sister was at home; the baby no doubt crying, and gurgling, and getting used to her new surroundings; and Chris and I chatting away, congratulating ourselves on how blessed we were to have two such beautiful little girls, with so many hopes for their futures.

Instead, we chatted about everything and nothing, just to pass the time. It helped, because, just for a little while, we didn't have to think. We could pretend that everything was ordinary and normal again, for a brief moment.

Yet, all the while, in truth our baby was never far from our hearts and minds.

That night, the events of the past few days would not leave my mind. I longed now for those baby movements that had been so difficult to cope with just a few nights ago. As I slept fitfully, on and off, I allowed my mind to focus on what I did have—my precious little Katie—and not on what I had lost. To have done anything else would have given me such deep emotional pain that I am not sure I could have borne it.

Morning finally came.

I could not remember having such a beautiful February day as this for a very long time. It felt as though spring was just around the corner and my spirit lifted as we made our way down to Devon. Though still very tired, I knew that this was right. I was so excited at seeing Katie, and couldn't wait to look once again into her big, blue eyes.

As we drove down the long driveway to Brunel Manor, butterflies filled my tummy at the thought of seeing everyone. It was a mixture of pleasure, and nervousness about how people would react.

I need not have worried, however.

As we walked into the huge entrance hall, with its grand fireplace and burning logs, I felt a real sense of welcome, and knew instinctively that we had done the right thing.

My parents and sister had been looking out for us. They immediately descended the long staircase to meet us. Dad was carrying Katie. Once down the stairs he put her down and she came giggling and running towards Chris and me. I scooped her up in my arms and buried my face in her hair, fighting back the tears so as not to upset her, but failing miserably. I explained that it was because I was so happy to see her.

Children are so very wonderful, aren't they? Within seconds, without drawing breath, she was rattling on about all that she had been doing with her Nan and Pop while we had been away.

My parents and sister let her chatter on, and then came forward to hug us. No words were spoken at that time.

None were needed.

We all carried the pain in our different ways.

Some grief is too hard to put into words. I was later to learn, as part of my child bereavement training, that learning to grieve without words can be a powerful resource. Words are often superfluous, and there are other ways to communicate our love and support.

After our initial greeting, my sister, Sue, took Katie off to play with the other children. Mum and Dad took us up to our room to make us a cup of tea. When we opened the door, the room was filled with the most beautiful flowers: roses, daisies, daffodils, and a variety of other flowers. The colours and the scent were so wonderful. We were overwhelmed with the beauty that the flowers had given to the room. On the table, there were cards from different members of our church family. Each one sensitively written. Each one bringing a tear to my eye; tears of gratitude for their love and thoughtfulness to us both.

There were times during that weekend when I wept, and wept.

So, was I right to go?

Most certainly.

Within that environment, all that people did was to love us. Often not with words, but with a listening ear, a caring look, a smile, or a hug. When you know people well, and you know they are genuine, that is all that you need. We weren't ignored because people didn't know what to say. We were embraced in other ways than words could express.

Love is such a funny thing, isn't it? When it is real, you just know. No one has to make a big deal about it. It just is.

And so it was with Elsie, a lady in her late sixties at the time. I had known Elsie for many years. She was a nursing sister at the hospital where I did my general training. She was also a member of my church. And, some years later, when Chris became the minister of the church we were now away with, she was a member there.

Elsie was unique.

She loved her Lord, and showed it by the way she lived her life for others. She was full of fun, and a tonic to be around. Even the young people had a soft spot for Elsie.

One of the loveliest things about her was that if she said she would pray for you, you knew it would be done. Such people used to be described as real 'prayer warriors.' Although it is now not such a fashionable saying, I like it, because it speaks of going into battle on behalf of others. And that is what I believe Elsie did.

I referred earlier to God's perfect timing regarding when my baby died. Let me explain further.

On the Sunday morning that we were at Brunel Manor, Chris led a communion service. It was a precious time together. Just after the service had finished, Elsie asked if she could see me. We walked in the lovely garden there, then sat down on one of the benches offering a lovely view of the grounds.

Elsie became very upset.

Before I knew it, she had tears flowing down her cheeks. I realised this had to be something that was really worrying her, as she was not one to weep easily, being of a more stoic nature. She apologised for her tears, explaining that she had a confession to make. I couldn't possibly imagine what this could be, but urged her to disclose it if she felt that it would help her.

Elsie proceeded to explain that, during the communion service, she had felt the Lord was constraining her to confess to me how she had let me down in my time of real need. She knew, if she didn't obey, she would have no peace. I listened, amazed at what she divulged.

Elsie had been at my parents' house, with others from our church, to pray for us while I was in labour. Later that evening, she went home, but couldn't sleep. She knew the Lord was telling her to get up and pray through the night for me. She did this. But, while she was kneeling by her bed, she started to feel sleepy. She made herself a cup of tea and began praying again. She related to me how she looked at her watch at six o'clock, and that was the last thing she could remember. She fell soundly asleep until nine.

She looked at me as though I should understand what her confession was. When she could see I didn't get it, she explained. Well, I failed you. The Lord asked me to pray for you through the night, and I fell asleep.

At that point, I put my arms around her and hugged her. 'O Elsie, you didn't fail me. In fact, your timing—and God's—was perfect. When you fell asleep was when I had the baby. You had prayed me through it all. She was born at six o'clock.'

We wept together, then.

I am quite sure that the Lord did not want her to share this with me as a confession, but as a wonderful testimony to His faithfulness, through prayer, and as an encouragement to us both.

Some may feel that God didn't answer Elsie's prayers, or those of others, that night, because the outcome was not a perfect child.

Who can fathom God's wisdom in these things?

Our baby did not live. But I did. Through a very difficult and traumatic birth.

Did Elsie's prayer make a difference?

As far as I am concerned, there is no doubt.

13

BURDENS AND BLESSINGS

The hardest thing about the weekend was going home.

It was such a lonely feeling, waving goodbye to everyone, feeling as though we were facing things on our own again. Of course, we weren't. It just felt like that. When I said goodbye to my parents, tears were in their eyes. I knew they felt as helpless as I did. I felt like a child again, vulnerable and afraid; needing them now as I had then, yet, equally, wanting Chris and I to have some time alone with one another, and with Katie, to adjust to all that had happened to us over the past four days.

When we walked through the door, I took some of the flowers from our room in Brunel Manor into the kitchen to rearrange, although I hardly had the heart for it. I remember putting the kettle on. This was a routine which, when you walked through the door in our house, was a given.

It was teatime for Katie. She sat munching away on her alphabetti spaghetti on toast, chatting non-stop about all that she had been doing with her cousins over the weekend. As I listened, I realised that I seemed to be saying yes and no in the right places, and smiling as she chatted on, whilst all I could think about was the empty room upstairs.

Our baby's nursery.

Chris came downstairs after unpacking our things. Seeing the look on my face, and knowing me as he did, he took over tea duty. The next thing I can recall was standing in the nursery and touching the different things we had bought for our new infant. As I did so, I began reminding myself how blessed we were to have such a lovely, healthy, lively, little girl downstairs. There were so many in our situation who didn't have another child to hold and love.

'Think again of what you have, not of what you have lost,' I chivvied myself. Yet, as my knees buckled and gave way, I crumpled in a heap to the floor. I couldn't count my blessings, despite the fact that it felt so wrong of me not to.

But the Lord knew my heart, and I could not lie. He understood. He would not hold this against me. Of that I was sure. And for that I was so very thankful. He wanted me to be honest, as a loving Father does.

I cried as though my heart would break.

People say that life goes on. Of course, that is true. We had love and support to help us through, although it was difficult, even for those closest to us, to know what to say or do to comfort us. The fact was that no one could make it better. No one could bring our daughter back to life. And right now, that was the only thing that could make it better.

Over the following weeks and months, well-meaning people sometimes tried to help by offering comments like, 'You are still young, and you can have another baby.' Or, 'You must be grateful. At least you already have a child.'

Others pointed out that time is a great healer, and we would soon move on from this.

You need to get on with your life.

Perhaps go back to work, to take your mind off things.

Look to the future.

One person even suggested that perhaps it was better that our baby had never breathed; that we hadn't got to know her. Maybe, they ventured, that made it easier in the long run. If she had lived, we would have had memories of her that would have been difficult to bear later.

It is no accident that this book's focus is precisely on looking at memories, and grieving, and the importance of both in the healing of our hearts and minds. There is undoubtedly some truth in many of the things that were, with good intention, communicated to us. However, when they trip off the tongue as platitudes—something to utter when people don't really know what to say, but feel they must say something—they are not always helpful, and can sometimes be hard to hear, however well-meaning and sincere.

I was, as I have said, so thankful for Katie. Yes, we could perhaps one day have another child. But no child could ever make up for the loss of this one. She was unique. Loved, and special—even in the womb—as only she could be. A gift from God, never to be simply replaced by another baby. Had our daughter lived, even for a few hours, there would at least have been some memories instead of this total, empty void that was never now to be filled.

I knew, or at least prayed, that I would not always feel this weight of grief upon me. Time was needed to bring healing. Not so that we could simply forget, and stop crying; but to learn to cry just because we missed her, and not out of the dark depths of raw and painful grieving. I firmly believe that there is a difference between the two. One cannot live with such a burden of grief forever. But neither can it simply be swept away. We have to learn to feel the pain, so that we can eventually break through it and find peace again.

Another not infrequent experience I had at that time was that some people would see me coming and, as surreptitiously as they could, walk the other way. Simply, I suspect, because they did not know what to say.

I am smiling as I write this, remembering what a dad at the Children's Hospice where I worked once shared with me, following the death of his six-month old baby. He recounted how he was in the supermarket and spotted his neighbour, whom he had known for years, across the aisle. He was sure that she had seen him. When she then turned and walked in the opposite direction, however, he assumed he had been mistaken.

He thought nothing more of it until he saw her again by the frozen food section. She looked towards him, and this time he knew she had seen him. As he was about to raise his hand in greeting once again, she turned and walked in the other direction.

He laughed as he related the story to me, because he then decided to follow her, finally cornering her by the bread and cakes. 'Hello,' he offered. 'Oh. . . Hi. . . I didn't see you there. . . .Well, I did see you, to be truthful. It's just that I didn't know what to say.' He told me that he simply replied, 'Don't worry. Next time, just come up and say, "I'm sorry. I just don't know what to say." That is so much more comforting than ignoring me, as I feel really isolated already.'

After hearing that story, I penned these simple words, for that Dad and for all who have maybe felt at some time as he did.

Please do not ignore me.
It's the hardest thing to bear,
when you will not look into my eyes,
and acknowledge she was there.

You do not have to worry
that your words may bring forth tears,
or that wrongly-worded sentences
will haunt me through the years.

And if your words are simply this:
'I don't know what to say,'
at least I'll know that someone's thoughts
have touched my life today.

But if you simply hurry by,
pretending I'm not there,
you merely add to the loneliness
that's already hard to bear.

So please don't be embarrassed
at the mention of her name,

for sharing makes her real again,
and helps to ease my pain.

You really cannot make it worse
by chatting for a while,
but maybe just a simple word
can give me back my smile.

So please do not ignore me.
It's the hardest thing to bear;
a smile, a word, reminds me
that others really care.

Most people, I have learned, are well-meaning and caring. When someone has lost a child, or has been bereaved in any way, it is hard to know how to react. It helps me to know that, on the whole, people do want to be supportive, but so often just don't know how. They want you to 'get better' quickly, so that they themselves can feel better, too.

I have probably heard it all, over the years, and I feel that it mostly comes down to well-meaning people being afraid of making it worse. I have learned, through my own experience, and that of working at the Hospice, that you can't actually make it worse.

This really is as bad as it gets.

I remember confiding in my sister, Sue, about how very alone I felt at times. She listened patiently, as she always did. The next day, I found a small envelope pushed through my door. Inside was a little card which read: 'I didn't really know what to say, but I saw this, and thought of you. I hope it helps.'

When the walls that surround you are silent,
and solitude weighs like a stone;
as you search for a shoulder to lean on,
just remember you're never alone.

When loneliness lowers its shadow
    and the voice that you hear is your own,
though nobody seems to be listening,
    remember you're never alone.
When each face in the street is a stranger,
    and the path that you tread is unknown,
be guided by faith and conviction,
    and remember you're never alone.
Whatever the doubts that assail you,
    however your dreams may be blown,
make Jesus your constant companion,
    and remember you're never alone.

I found those words so comforting, and I was reminded once more that when we feel lonely—and that can even be, in fact sometimes more so, when we are in a crowd, when people don't know what to say, or how to approach us, we are not on our own. For Jesus is our constant companion.

I was to learn that grieving does not always run through neat stages.

We are individuals, and so we grieve individually. We will not always react as others think we should. Or, in fact, even how we think we will. Grieving really means expressing all the emotions and feelings that we have at a time of loss in our lives. It means slowly accepting the awful reality, and the pain of what has happened, but also learning day by day to begin to live with the changes that have taken place in our lives.

Grieving is never simply about moving on, forgetting the person who has died. Rather, it is about finding a permanent place for them in your life. A place that doesn't cause you constant pain, for such depths of pain would be impossible to live with on a permanent basis.

Time alone cannot heal.

If only it were that simple, we could just wait.

Grieving involves working through the pain, in order to

come through the other side. Sadly, there is no short-cut to feeling better after losing anyone we have truly loved.

So often, while working at the Hospice, I felt myself powerless. Helpless. Frustrated by what seemed like my inability to take away a parent's pain. I could sit and weep with them, and hold their hand. But I couldn't reach inside and mend their broken heart. I couldn't simply replace their child with another one, as you would replace a broken toy for a toddler.

There is, in fact, no bandage or plaster large enough to mend what has been broken. I could not join them in the loneliness of their grief. And, as tight as my arms could hold them, I could never touch that inner pain and isolation.

Where could I find the right words to bring comfort? Or advice, to save them from one more day's pain? All the books and wisdom in the world could not offer the peace they now craved.

I could hold a cold, damp cloth to their swollen eyes, but it would not remove the reason for their tears. I could whisper over and over that it would be alright, hoping that they would believe it, yet knowing really that they wouldn't. Couldn't. The death of a loved one takes you down a hard and lonely path.

One of the most important and valuable gifts we can offer someone at such a time is to listen. And to listen. And to listen. To listen through the lack of acceptance, the pain, the fear, the guilt, the anger and recriminations, the helplessness, the lack of confidence and concentration, the physical symptoms and panic as at times they feel they will go mad with grief. These experiences can be so terrifying. And these are but a few of the reactions that may become a new and frightening part of person's life when they are grieving.

The right kind of support is so important at such a time as this. To hang in there with someone is a big commitment. But the opportunity to share with someone that you trust to be there for the long haul can make such a difference.

If we take time to listen to someone's concerns, even though we may not fully understand them—for each person's experience of grief and pain is unique—we can begin to have some understanding of their situation, and thereby learn how to support them in the best way.

That best way is not always in speaking. Or even listening. But, sometimes, in doing.

I remember one woman who described her particular experience to me. She was very close to her friends in the neighbourhood, yet, in the early days after her three year old son died suddenly, and tragically, in an accident, both she and her husband found it so hard even to talk to these neighbours and friends.

She recounted how precious it was, during that difficult period, when a knock would come at the front door and when, on answering, she would find the caller gone, but a cake, a casserole, or sometimes some shopping, left at her door. This continued not just for a few days, but for weeks.

Eventually, she had the confidence to resume those friendships again. She was able to do so because, as she explained to me, although she hadn't wanted, or been able, to talk to them, they had never given up on her. This made it so much easier to approach them, and to renew the friendships, once she and her husband were ready.

A few years ago, I came across story. It is a true story that really touched my heart. There was a flight boarding at London Heathrow for New York. Everyone was clambering to get on board, including a young mother and her three children, aged eighteen months, three and five years old. The flight was delayed and the children were already becoming restless, even before the flight took off. The fight attendant came around with colouring books and crayons in an endeavour to occupy the children.

Eventually the flight took to the air. Whilst there were a fair number of children on board the flight that day, it was this young mother's children that were drawing the attention. They were constantly crying, or bickering with one another. And the mother made little attempt to quieten them. After about an hour had passed, food was brought around. But still the children continued to be unsettled and factious.

Finally, one of the other passengers decided that he had had enough, and he complained to the flight attendant. She spoke kindly to the mother, asking her to try and keep the little ones quieter. The young mum apologised, promising that she would.

However, nothing changed.

As time passed, some of the passengers began to grumble to one another, observing what an awful mother she was. Her children seemed out of control, whilst she just sat there like a zombie, not even trying to discipline them. She really should have some consideration for all of the other passengers around her.

Since there were still several hours of the flight to go, one of the passengers finally reproached her, requesting in fairly strong terms that she control her children as they were ruining the flight for everyone around them. At this, the young mother burst into tears and began sobbing uncontrollably.

The passenger, now feeling rather embarrassed, asked her what was wrong. She began to relate her story. The previous day, she had received a phone call from the construction company in New York for which her husband had been working for the past three months. It had been a wonderful opportunity for him, and indeed for them as a family. For she and the children were to join him, after six months, to live there together.

The phone call had changed everything.

She was given the tragic news that her husband had been involved in a terrible accident. He had fallen from scaffolding on one of the high-rise buildings and was in a coma, being kept alive only by a life-support machine.

He was brain dead. Tragically, there was no hope of him regaining consciousness.

She was on her way to New York to give permission, as his next of kin, to turn off the life-support machine. 'I am so sorry,' she sobbed, 'that the children have been naughty. Usually they are so good. I just can't seem to function very well. I guess it must be the shock.'

After hearing her story, those in the seats around her all went quiet, not knowing what to say. Then, after a few moments, people went into action. Someone informed the flight attendant, who brought her and the children a drink. A young man and his wife let the five year old sit with their little girl and play some games. An elderly lady sat and held the young mum's hand, while some of the other passengers coloured books and entertained the three-year old. By now, the one-year old was asleep on her mummy's lap.

Suddenly, everything, and everyone's attitude, had changed.

Why?

Because someone had listened.

In listening, he had come to understand the situation. As a result, for the next five hours people had supported her. The young mother's tragic circumstances had sadly not changed. However, for those brief, all-important moments she had been given respite—in this case from strangers who, throughout the rest of the flight, were there for her.

Isn't human nature wonderful?

So often, when the chips are down, there is someone on whom we can rely. People are so important in our lives. Yet, there is an even greater presence: our Heavenly Father. I have learned that there is never a moment, if we are open to Him, that He will not be there for us. Our circumstances may be dire, but God will remain steadfast, loving and kind throughout the whole of this life's journey, and beyond.

He, too, is in it for the long haul.

At the end of our first full day back at home, we tucked

Katie into bed and said a prayer with her. She grinned, clapped her hands, and shouted a loud 'Amen' at the end. We then sang with her a little chorus that was a favourite of hers. Wriggling back out of bed, she of course had to do the actions. The words went:

Two little eyes to look to God,
two little ears to hear His Word,
two little lips to sing His praise,
two little feet to walk in His ways,
two little hands to do His will,
and one little heart to love Him still.

How we loved singing along, watching Katie doing the actions. When we reached the end, there were the inevitable shouts of 'More. More.' As we tucked her into bed again, it struck me for the first time that the little chorus that we had been singing seemed to speak of wholeness, and the giving of ourselves back to God. Our eyes and ears, hands, feet, and lips, given back to Him in worship.

A feeling of overwhelming sadness enveloped me as I realised that our baby could never worship Him in that way, for she had not been whole when she was born.

In fact, quite the opposite.

However, comfort then came through these words from Psalm 139 (vv.13-18).

For you created my inmost being;
* you knit me together in my mother's womb.*
I praise you because I am fearfully and wonderfully made;
* your works are wonderful,*
* I know that full well.*
My frame was not hidden from you
* when I was made in the secret place.*
When I was woven together in the depths of the earth,
* your eyes saw my unformed body.*

All the days ordained for me
  were written in your book
  before one of them came to be.
How precious to me are your thoughts, God!
  How vast is the sum of them!
Were I to count them,
  they would outnumber the grains of sand.
When I awake,
  I am still with you.

I knew that what God was saying to me was that He was in control. He may have allowed this to happen, but our baby's life had still been precious to Him.

He had created her.

His eyes had seen her unformed body, and He ordained all her days. When she awoke, it was never meant to be with us, but with Him, where her wholeness would be complete, and she could worship Him throughout eternity.

God had created her from us, and had given us nine wonderful months of loving and nurturing her. Our daughter may not have been physically healed, but she is more that just physical matter. She has a soul, which cannot be touched by physical imperfections. She was a gift, and was never meant to live in this world, but in heaven with Him.

This has given me so much comfort over the years. After all, even for us this is not all that there is.

There is far more—and better—to come!

The following morning, I was up before Chris, which was unusual. I had woken with the awful realisation that she wasn't there: in my tummy; in her little cot; in our lives. I went into the bathroom and threw some water on my face. As I looked into the mirror, I was aware that my eyes stared back at me, looking swollen and dead. I felt the now all-too-familiar feeling of anxiety and panic creeping over me, so I went down stairs to put the kettle on.

As I sat drinking my tea, and staring out of the window, I

heard little feet on the stairs. I went and watched as our bleary-eyed, tousled-haired little girl came down the stairs. My heart was overwhelmed with a love that only a parent can really understand. I picked her up. Despite trying not to get upset, I sobbed into her curls. Her chubby little arms tightened around my neck.

Just for one moment—it was the only time it ever happened—I imagined that they were her sister's. The tears ran unchecked down my cheeks. 'Mummy sad,' she volunteered. 'Yes,' I replied, 'but hugging you has helped Mummy.' And it truly had.

Katie patted my back, as an adult might do to comfort a child. It was her unique little thing that she did. When she saw me smiling, she asked if she could pat her baby now.

I realised how much I had dreaded her mentioning the baby. It suddenly struck me that although we had talked about the baby coming soon, Katie had never once in the past four days asked anything about her. She hadn't seemed to pick up on any of the sadness around her. This was largely due, I was sure, to the love, prayer and support that had surrounded her over the past few days. I believe that God, in His infinite wisdom, had given us much-needed space.

After we had included Katie as much as possible in the prospect and anticipation of the new baby, I worried now how she was going to cope with the disappointment of not having a brother or sister.

After her remark about patting the baby, I realised that, even at her young age, Katie needed an explanation.

But when?

I didn't want to worry or frighten her. I knew that we needed wisdom in how, and when, to broach this with her.

Later that day, we were playing with Katie when she suddenly, while continuing to put shapes in her shape-sorter, asked, 'Mummy, where's the baby?' Tears immediately sprang to my eyes. Trying once again to control them, I lost the fight. I gulped them back and gave her my brightest, watery smile.

Chris was sat on the floor, and stared at me, as if to say, 'We didn't see that coming.' I picked Katie up onto my lap, searching for the right way to communicate that we needed to tell her something very sad. The baby would not be coming to live with us after all.

As I looked into her innocent, expressive, blue eyes, I knew that I wanted to protect her from all of life's troubles and sadnesses. I offered a quiet prayer that she would know God's love and protection as she grew up, to face whatever life may throw at her.

I explained to Katie that the baby had gone to heaven to live with Jesus. 'Will it come another day?' she asked, still playing with her toy. 'No.' I replied, 'The baby will live with Jesus forever, but will be very happy.' She looked up at me, then. And, in a sad little voice which tore at my heart, simply emitted a sound that reflected her disappointment. She knew about heaven already; that it was a very special and nice place, where Jesus was. Very young as she still was, this explanation seemed to be enough.

Later that day, my parents came to visit us, laden with flowers, goodies for us to eat, and a colouring book and crayons for Katie. Dad helped her draw a picture of a cow whilst Mum and I chatted in the kitchen.

Later, while we were all having a cup of tea and some cake, Katie suddenly blurted out, 'The baby's not coming here anymore. It's gone to live in heaven. Jesus is looking after it for us.' We all looked at each other with a mixture of tears and smiles. To Katie, it was as simple as that.

The faith and trust of a child. Quite extraordinary, isn't it?

Several times in the following weeks the subject was to come up, but Katie seemed content that her baby, as she called it, was safe with Jesus. As far as she was concerned, there was nothing to fear.

The child had become a blessing to her burdened parents. And when, over the years, life has been tough, she has continued to be so.

❋ 14 ❋

THE INVISIBLE MASK

As I have noted before, life is made up of meetings and partings. And when new people arrive in our lives for the first time, we never know the impact that they may have.

Her name was Bernie, and she was a midwife with years of experience. She was Irish. As soon as she opened her mouth, there was no doubting that fact. Since coming out of hospital, I had seen a midwife several times, which was the norm in those days.

For the next visit my usual midwife was on holiday. Bernie had been sent instead. She was as tall as she was round, and was larger than life. She had a happy face that beamed a great smile as soon as she walked through the door. It was hard to feel sad when Bernie was around. I guess you could say she was an extravert. Not in an overbearing way, but in a way that communicated that if you had a problem she would be the one to help you sort it.

I made a cup of tea, and we sat for a while and chatted. She made it so easy, and asked me if I minded sharing with her what had happened over the past few weeks. I didn't mind, so I began. I remember feeling rather surprised, since the other midwife seemed simply to glean her information from my notes.

As I related my story to her, I felt for the first time that here was someone in the medical profession to whom I could really talk easily about our baby. I soon realised that his wasn't just a job to her. It was much more. I chatted for about half an hour, then she checked me out physically and confirmed all was going well. She reminded me that in four weeks I would go back to the hospital for my final check-up.

As Bernie was leaving, she suggested that she come back for one final visit. I was surprised by this, but more than happy for her to return. So we arranged it for the following week.

Two weeks had passed since our baby had died.

The following week, like the two previous ones, was lived in rather a getting-through-it-because-I-had-to kind of way. My life took on something of its old routine again, and every day I expected it to get easier.

But it didn't.

We decided to put the baby's things away in the loft. It was just too distressing to look at them. Chris was so gentle and patient with me, but he was at as much as a loss as I was. My family were loving and supportive, but somehow nothing seemed to ease the aching void and sense of loss.

During that time, my breasts were leaking, despite tablets to try and prevent it. Whenever I thought of my baby feeding, it only served to make it worse. I longed to hold her to my breast. To feel that wonderful skin-to-skin contact that is so special between mother and child. This also further highlighted in my own mind and heart that I had failed as a mother, with the result that at times I felt that I was spiralling out of control.

When I went out, or saw anyone, I would reach for my invisible mask, as I thought of it, and put it on. The mask that would smile and say, 'I'm OK. I'm getting there. Don't worry about me. I'm coping.' I felt that I must show to the world—especially my non-Christian friends—how my faith was holding me up, keeping me going. I felt a sense of guilt if, for a moment, I conveyed otherwise. It was as though I was letting God down.

I also felt that, even though I wanted to, I mustn't keep talking about it. It just wasn't fair. It would only upset people, if I did that.

But when I was alone . . . that's when it hit me.

There were times, when I prayed, that I felt as though my

prayers simply hit the ceiling. Then I reminded myself of what a dear Minister had once declared to me, many years before. 'Oh, not to worry. God is also below the ceiling.' And yet my faith was suddenly starting to feel like something of an act. Not that I blamed God, or loved Him less. I clung desperately on to Him.

But still, I felt isolated from everything and everybody.

The empty void in my life at that time is not easy to describe in any way that makes sense. I felt so battered by despair. It was as though someone had turned off all the lights. There was such a mixture of emotion that I wrestled to understand, but it was simply beyond my comprehension.

So I sought to fill those first few weeks with doing things. The busier my life was, the less I would have to think. And yet, even in my busy-ness, or when I was chatting to Chris, or my family, it was as though there were two conversations occurring at the same time in my head. Even whilst doing the very thing that I loved so very much, playing with Katie —even then, our baby dominated my thoughts constantly.

I read my Bible. But even that felt more of a duty than joy. And so I felt guilty again. I felt like a hamster in a wheel, just rolling around and around and coming up against the same obstacles time and time again.

The waves of grief felt so intense it was frightening. I felt as though they would overwhelm me at times. But they did not. For the Lord knows just how much we can take, and His strength is given just when we need it. Help came in an unexpected way a few days later, when Bernie came to visit again.

When I was around ten years old, our family went to buy a puppy. He had a beautiful black, curly coat and big, dark brown liquid eyes. When he had been naughty and looked up at us, as much as to say, 'Please don't be cross with me,' it made it very difficult to chastise him.

He had abnormally long ears, which was one of the reasons we fell in love with him. They were so long we had to tie them back when he was eating, and he looked really comical. In fact, he had ears that Dumbo the Elephant would have been proud of!

Bo, as we named him, was cute and funny and, along with my sister, I used to teach him tricks. Where we lived at that time there was a long corridor with a shiny floor. We taught Bo to run, sit down, and then slide along the floor on his rear end until he came to a stop at the glass door at the end of the corridor. He would then get some doggy treats for performing so well.

One day we had a family outing to a beautiful old castle in Warwickshire. My sister and I had a wonderful time, running around the grounds, letting our imaginations run wild. The castle was partly a ruin and was a wonderful spot for kids to play.

After a while, we went inside and walked up to the tower, three floors up. We knew that there would be wonderful views across the grounds to admire. I had Bo on his lead and, as usual, he was quite content to walk beside me. As we walked through the door at the top, the empty room stretched before us, as did the old wooden floor, made shiny by the thousands of feet that had walked on it over the years.

As we stepped into the room, Bo took one look at the floor and pulled away from me on his lead. Sure enough, he ran, sat down, and went sliding towards the enormous floor-to-ceiling window on the other side of the room. It looked very funny. Except for the fact that there was no glass in the window. As we raced after him, screaming out and trying to catch him, we realised to our horror that it was too late.

He went flying out of the window and began to fall to the ground beneath.

We covered the three fights of stairs from the tower as fast as our legs would carry us, sobbing as we went, knowing in our hearts that there was no way he could survive such a fall. As we emerged through the door that led to the gravel path that surrounded the castle, we saw a few people standing in a little group. We ran over to them, still crying, dreading what they, and we, would have to witness.

To our utter amazement, there he was, lying quite unperturbed in a baby's pram!

We were now laughing and crying, all at the same time, enquiring what had happened. A young woman explained that she had taken the baby out of the pram not ten minutes before. As they walked along, she had been chatting away to her Mum when she felt a thud in the pram. When she looked, she had the surprise of her life. There was Bo!

After checking he was all right, and thanking her profusely, Dad took us all for a much-needed cup of tea. We were so grateful that our little dog was safe; but also that the baby had been removed from her pram when she had. What a miracle!

When I have related that story to friends over the years, it has always served as a visual reminder to me that, for us as Christians, God has promised that underneath us are the everlasting arms. His arms. Even when we feel ourselves hurtling towards the abyss, He will protect us from the hard ground beneath. Sometimes we do find ourselves in free-fall, but He never loses sight of us. And it has been my experience that He will catch us, and hold on to us. Even in our moments of greatest pain.

He lifts us up again from the dark place of grief, and we can take our refuge in Him. Then, once again, He continues with us on our journey. In Psalm 61:2-4, we read:

> *From the ends of the earth I call to you,*
>   *I call as my heart grows faint;*
>   *lead me to the rock that is higher than I.*
> *For you have been my refuge,*
>   *a strong tower against the foe.*
> *I long to dwell in your tent forever*
>   *and take refuge in the shelter of your wings.*

I was putting the kettle on, ready for coffee, when the doorbell rang. I knew that it would be Bernie. I was looking forward to seeing her again. She came into the kitchen with me and asked about Chris and Katie. Chris was working at the church, and Katie was at my parents' for the morning. So I knew that she would be having all of their attention lavished on her. I had bought us some chocolate biscuits. It felt as though a friend was visiting, rather than the just the midwife. And my spirits were lifted slightly.

Bernie enquired how my week had been, and how I was feeling. Of course, I smiled and indicated that I was fine. No problems.

I looked down into my cup, expecting her to say something like, 'OK, that's good.' But there was silence. After a while, I looked up at her. She was looking straight at me. 'You know,' she offered, 'it is safe to take the mask off with me. But only if you want to.' I shall never forget the look of compassion on her face.

For a moment, I just stared at her.

How did she know?

I hadn't divulged those thoughts about my invisible mask to anyone.

It was then that the floodgates opened, and I sobbed. She didn't reach out to touch me. She simply sat. And as the tears ceased, I knew that there were three of us in that room, not two.

I opened up my heart to her that morning, and it all came tumbling out. And as I spoke, she simply listened, until I had poured out all of my disappointment, guilt, anger, and pain. I protested to her that the loss of our baby seemed such a terrible waste of a life, with all its potential. All our suffering was for nothing. I also acknowledged that I felt so tired and weary—physically, emotionally, and spiritually. Although I felt that I should be able to cope, I continued, I knew that, in all honesty, I wasn't. There were times, when I thought of my baby being born so damaged, that I felt as though my heart would break.

What was the sense in it all?

Bernie suggested that maybe it was time to take off the mask. To give myself permission to share with others the pain and grief that I was experiencing. To trust my own instincts, as the days went by, of how much to open up to those I could trust and be completely honest with. Those who loved me didn't expect me to be 'brave' and get over it in five minutes. And those who did have such expectations weren't important. They simply didn't get it, was how she put it.

She counselled me not to concern myself about upsetting others by being more open. She reminded me that those who loved me were already upset. Perhaps opening up to them was offering them a gift: the opportunity to give me much-needed love and support. In so giving, they too might be comforted.

Bernie asked me about my faith. She had seen a lovely wooden plaque on our wall, which read:

'I asked Jesus, "How much do you love me?"
He said, "This much."
And He stretched out His arms, and died.'

She drew my attention to it. I sobbed once more as I explained how I had come to faith many years before. She informed me that she was a Roman Catholic. Although she had learned that she never had to put on the mask where God was concerned, she had on many occasions felt the need to put it on for other people. This was something that, emotionally, had cost her dearly over the years.

Bernie went on to relate to me the story of a woman she knew who, years before, had lost a baby girl in similar circumstances to ourselves. On one occasion, someone had observed what a waste their unborn baby's life was. This had caused the mother great distress. She was left wondering, 'So, what was the point in all this suffering?'

She had gone to her Priest. He reflected with her that when an elderly person dies, their life is often looked back upon and measured by relationships made, and by the things they had done and achieved. Their life was celebrated for those things, and rightly so.

He then pointed out to her that although her baby had only lived for a short amount of time, she had been made in the image of God. She had been nourished, and had developed. She had known what it was to be dependent on her mother, who gave her unconditional love while she was in the womb. That baby had experienced real love, in the deepest sense of the word.

The Priest, Bernie explained, showed the young mother that these were the memories she could carry with her. That no child's life that was remembered could ever be seen as a waste. He reminded her that Jesus promises us that He has gone to prepare a place for us, teaching us that life is not just about the here and now, and offering eternal life.

The Priest assured the woman that her daughter had not been taken from her for nothing. Moreover, she was now living her life in God's presence. He comforted her by helping her to see that her daughter had not left this life with disappointment, or regrets, or things left undone, as so many do. She was now safe, and would never be touched by life's pain or tears. Although, yes, she had been born so physically damaged, her soul was not.And she was now sharing her sweetness with Jesus in heaven.

While Bernie was relating this story, Viktor Frankl's words, which I quoted in an earlier chapter, came back to me: 'We cannot judge a biography by its length, or by the number of pages in it. We must judge it by the richness of its content. Sometimes the "unfinished" are among the most beautiful of the symphonies.'

As Bernie spoke to me, I felt sure that it must have been

her own child she was referring to. She relayed that conversation so very clearly, there was really no doubt in my mind to whom the Priest had been talking. As a professional, she had not dumped her own stuff on me, but had conveyed her experience in an anonymous way, to help and gently challenge. Her empathic and sympathetic responses to me came, I believe, out of her own heart of pain.

When I asked her, 'Do you believe that such sadness can be overcome, and eventually be used to help others?' she simply smiled, and replied, 'In some cases, yes. For God doesn't waste even our most painful experiences. It's a question of whether we are prepared to let Him work through us to use them, when the time is right. But it takes courage and faith to do so.'

Bernie's final act was to leave me with a passage of Scripture that she felt might be a help and encouragement to me. It was Hebrews 12: 11-13.

> *'No discipline seems pleasant at the time, but painful. Later on, however, it produces a harvest of righteousness and peace for those who have been trained by it. Therefore, strengthen your feeble arms and weak knees! "Make level paths for your feet," so that the lame may not be disabled, but rather healed.'*

I hugged Bernie as she was leaving. I told her that I believed the Lord had sent her to me. She was a complete stranger when she first came to my door. It was years later that I heard someone say that no time is wasted that makes two people friends. Bernie had come as a stranger, and had left as a friend.

God's angel sent in my time of need.

After she had gone, I went to my bedroom and wrote down the things we had shared that morning, not wanting to forget them. I opened the window and, as I did so, the breeze blew the curtain back and knocked over my guitar, which was standing nearby, in the corner. As I picked it up, I was reminded of the day that I had bought it, and I smiled to myself.

At the time, I was living in Birmingham, training to be a midwife. I loved to sing, and was learning to play the guitar so that I could use it at church. I had been saving up for this particular instrument for over a year as it was a particularly good one, and quite expensive. I had had the guitar for several weeks, and it stood proudly on a stand in the corner of my room. Whenever I walked in, it was the first thing I would notice. Made of beautiful wood, the front was carved in a simple design that was quite unique to that particular make.

It was so splendid I was almost afraid to start playing it, as I didn't want to spoil it. It was such a treasured possession.

As I was chiding myself for being silly—what was the use of it just sitting there?—there was a knock on the door. A member of my church stood there. He was in the neighbourhood, he informed me, and thought he'd pop in for a cup of coffee.

Despite what followed, he was to become one of my dearest friends in the years to come. His name was Chris. He and his wife Pauline led the youth work in our church. They were such dear people, and they cared for us all as though we were family. I shall never forget their love and kindness to me while I was living away from my home.

I showed Chris my new treasured possession, with pride. He was delighted that I had finally got it. He was himself an excellent guitarist; much more accomplished than I. He asked if I would like him to tune it for me as the keys were quite stiff, and I was struggling to turn them.

He went back to his car, and came back with a small pair of pliers. As he was turning the final one, I felt so excited, and couldn't wait to play it. Then, lifting the pliers for the final time, they suddenly slipped from his hand. They dropped on top of the guitar, leaving a dent in the beautiful wood.

The room was silent.

We just stared at the damage, and then at each other.

Looking at Chris's face, all thoughts of the damaged guitar went from my head. He was mortified. I heard myself say, 'Chris, it doesn't matter. It was just an accident. It won't stop me being able to play it.'

Although I loved my guitar, his feelings were for me more important. Of course, I never let him forget it! Yet, I would regularly follow my playful chastisements with the assurance that although the body was damaged, it still had the sweetest sound.

What a wonderfully timely reminder this memory was for me that day in my bedroom. It would have been easy to leave the guitar sitting there, looking pretty, but being unused, and therefore lifeless. It was its sound that gave it life. Bernie had encouraged me with the thought that, in similar fashion, although our baby's body was so damaged, she was now sharing her sweetness with Jesus.

Not long after Bernie's visit, I read an article that reminded me of that day and I was greatly blessed by the recollection that the article prompted.

My brother-in-law opened the bottom drawer of my sister's bureau and lifted out a tissue-wrapped package. 'This,' he said, 'is not a slip. This is lingerie.' He discarded the tissue and handed me the slip. It was exquisite: silk, handmade, and trimmed with a cobweb of lace. The price tag, with an astronomical figure on it, was still attached. 'Jan bought this the first time that we went to New York, at least eight or nine years ago. She never wore it. She was saving it for a special occasion. Well, I guess this is the occasion.'

He took the slip from me, and put it on the bed with the other things that we were taking to the mortician. His hands lingered on the soft material for a moment, then he slammed the door shut and turned to me. 'Don't ever save anything for a special occasion. Every day you're alive is a special occasion.'

Those words changed my life, and I'm trying very hard not to put things off, hold back, or save anything that would add laughter and lustre to our lives. And, every morning, when I open my eyes, I tell myself that it is special. Every day, every minute, every breath, truly is a gift.

(Anne Wells, *source unknown*)

Bernie's conversation with me that day, and the helpful insights she offered, was a gift from God. The chances were that I would never see Bernie again. And, in fact, I never did. However, I have never forgotten her. How could I?

As I walked out of my bedroom, it was three weeks after the death of our baby. I felt for the first time hopeful again.

And, there and then, I made a conscious decision to remove the mask, and give it to God.

15

GO FOR IT!

Chris came with me for my six-week check at the local hospital. All was well. We were advised that there was no reason not to go ahead with another pregnancy, in time, but that there was a one-in-twenty chance that this could happen to us again. This was unexpected and disturbing news, to say the least. Nevertheless, if we decided to try again, we would face things together—and just one step at a time.

We went for a coffee on our way home, at a local garden centre. Spring was almost upon us and there were blossoms on the trees. Despite the shock we had just received at the hospital, we both felt hopeful.

As we sat drinking our coffee, we chatted about our recent visit to Yorkshire to see Chris's parents. It seemed the right time to let him know something His Mum had disclosed to me during that visit; namely, that she had had a stillbirth some years after his youngest brother, Ian, had been born.

Although this would have been her sixth child, she reflected how it didn't in any way take away the pain and loss of that one. I started to cry, and she just put her arms around me. She didn't say anything, except, 'It's alright, lass.' Once again, there was no real need for words. Just the fact that I knew she felt my pain because of her own, on that day many years ago.

And I was comforted.

Chris had not even been aware that his Mum had lost a baby. In those days, even less than in ours, you simply got on with it. In many families, some things were simply not discussed and you didn't openly lay bare your grief, or whatever other feelings you might be struggling with. I was grateful, and felt privileged, that she had chosen to share with me this very personal and private experience.

How my heart ached for her.

Chris and I considered together the possibility that perhaps in the future God would smile upon us again, as He had with Katie, and we might perhaps one day have another baby.

Before my conversation with Bernie, this would have felt like a betrayal of our baby who had died. But today it didn't. The story she told, and her wise counsel, had stayed with me. I knew that although our little girl could never be replaced, for us to have another child, and for Katie to have a little brother or sister, would be a blessing, and not simply a replacement.

Later that day, we prayed, and thanked God that I was OK, and asked Him for wisdom in discerning our future direction. I was wondering about going back to work in a few months, maybe in a part time capacity. One or two shifts a week at our local hospital would be enough.

I had very mixed feelings.

I was a little afraid of the prospect of being around newborn babies again so soon. I knew that I was still standing on wobbly ground. But perhaps being back at work in the profession I had so enjoyed would encourage me, and give me the confidence I needed to step out into the world again. Maybe, even—although this felt scary—I would have the opportunity to testify to staff there that I already knew God's goodness in getting me through this difficult time.

If I were to take this step, I knew it would take courage. And, to be honest, I wasn't sure that I possessed it. Before I went to bed that night my daily reading was from 2 Corinthians 4. It was verses 5-9 and 16-18 that leapt out at me on that occasion.

For what we preach is not ourselves, but Jesus Christ as Lord,
and ourselves as your servants for Jesus' sake. For God, who
said, 'Let light shine out of darkness,' made his light shine in
our hearts to give us the light of the knowledge of God's glory
displayed in the face of Christ. But we have this treasure in
jars of clay to show that this all–surpassing power is from
God and not from us. We are hard pressed on every side, but
not crushed; perplexed, but not in despair; persecuted, but not
abandoned; struck down, but not destroyed.' . . . Therefore we
do not lose heart. Though outwardly we are wasting away, yet
inwardly we are being renewed day by day. For our light and
momentary troubles are achieving for us an eternal glory that
far outweighs them all. So we fix our eyes not on what is seen,
but on what is unseen, since what is seen is temporary, but
what is unseen is eternal.

Feeling like a very ordinary, and extremely battered, jar of
clay, I asked myself whether His light could really still shine
out from me, after all that had happened.

These verses gave me a new confidence.

Yes, I was standing on very shaky legs at the moment.
Nevertheless, I need not lose heart. I had only to fix my eyes
upon Him. If I did, I would not, and in fact could not, be
destroyed.

When I was a child, we would sometimes go to the circus.
Wow. What amazing acts! Among my favourites were the
trapeze and the high wire acts. Had there not been a safety
net to catch the brave performers in the event they fell, I
would probably not have been as keen. Yet, even as a young
child, I knew, in the unlikely event that they did fall, they
would come to no harm.

I now understood, should I start to wobble and fall, that
God would be my safety net.

To draw on another childhood memory, when I was a
very little girl my Dad would put a record on the
gramophone player and ask me to dance with him. He would

bow, and I would curtsey. I would then stand on his feet, and we would dance. We would twirl round and round the room until the record stopped. Had he let go of me for just one moment, I would have fallen for sure. However, I was never anxious. Why? Because I knew that he would never let go. I had faith that he would not—although I didn't understand it as faith, then. It was simply that my Dad had never given me any reason to doubt him.

God had not abandoned me.

I was not destroyed.

He had given me no reason not to trust Him.

Furthermore, He had promised to renew me day by day.

That night, I prayed for renewed courage to face the next step. Even after this encouragement, however, I was well aware that that next step might not be easy.

The next six weeks went by quickly.

I had sent off for the application forms for a job that fitted the hours I felt able to do. I still had a toddler at home, but these hours fitted in very well with Chris's work, so that he would able to look after Katie while I was at work. When the forms arrived, I filled them in with a feeling of excitement and anticipation.

This was it.

I was getting out of the boat.

Would I walk, or sink?

That was the question.

A week later, I had a letter offering me an interview. Instead of feeling excited, I was terrified. My mind was filled with questions like, What am I doing? Am I really ready yet? Is it too soon? After all, it had only been three months since our baby had died. Why not wait a while? There's no rush.

I knew that in reality I was trying to convince myself. But there was a persistent whisper in my head that this was the right time, and not to wait. I rang the hospital and confirmed that I would be attending for the interview and was delighted to have the opportunity.

I wasn't delighted, truth be told. Nonetheless, it sounded like the right response. Anyway, even if offered the job, I could still turn it down, couldn't I?

The following day, I went for coffee with my sister, Sue. One of the things I loved about her was that she always told it as it was. Good common sense. No messing. Yet always served up with a generous helping of love.

I divulged my anxieties about the job, in response to which she smiled. She then launched straight in. 'It seems to me as though you're trying to talk yourself out of it. You only get one shot at life. You need to seize it with both hands. What if this is God's time, and the right timing for this particular job, and you miss it? It would be a shame to look back with regrets.'

I knew she was right.

As we separated, she gave me a great big hug, as she whispered softly, 'You can do it.' I thanked God for her honesty in not simply telling me what I wanted to hear. 'Don't do it. It's much too soon. Run a mile.'

Nonetheless, had I decided not to take the opportunity, I knew that she would have supported me in that decision as well. That's the kind of sister she is. However, as I walked away, I knew that I would seize the moment, albeit with fear, and trepidation.

I could do this.

And, yes. I got the job.

Some years later, a friend gave me a photocopy of some words that had been written by a lady called Emma Bombeck, who had died of cancer. Beyond that, I knew nothing of her circumstances.

The copy was very faded, but I was just able to make out the words. I was so glad that I did.

My invisible suitcase popped open again.

Whilst reading the words, I recalled my conversation with Sue.

If I had my life to live over
I would have talked less and listened more.
I would have invited friends over to dinner, even if the carpet was stained and the sofa faded.
I would have eaten the popcorn in the 'GOOD' living room and worried much less about the dirt when someone wanted to light a fire in the fireplace.
I would have taken the time to listen to my grandfather ramble on about his youth.
I would never have insisted that the car windows be rolled up on a summer's day because my hair had just been set and sprayed.
I would have burned the pink candle sculpted like a rose before it melted in storage.
I would have sat on the lawn with my children and not worried about grass stains.
I would have cried and laughed less while watching television, and more while watching life.
I would have gone to bed when I was sick instead of pretending the earth would go into a holding pattern if I weren't there for a day.
I would never have bought anything just because it was practical, wouldn't show the dirt or was guaranteed to last a lifetime.
Instead of wishing away nine months of pregnancy, I'd have cherished every moment, realising that the wonderment that was growing inside me was the only chance in life to assist God in a miracle.
When my kids kissed me impetuously, I would never have said, 'Later. Now go get washed for dinner.'
There would have been more 'I love you,' and more 'I'm sorry.'
But mostly, given another shot at life, I would seize every moment. Look at it, and really see it. Live it and never give it back.

I was so touched by Emma's words.

How thankful I was that, through His strength, I had been able to seize the day and take the job. Had I not, I would not have had opportunities I was presented with to share God's love. Or to empathise, drawing on the experience of losing my own baby, with others whose hearts were breaking.

Was I filled with doubts and fears, initially?

Of course.

Absolutely no regrets, though.

I began working as a staff midwife for two shifts a week. Many of the staff I already knew. They were aware of what had happened to our baby, and were kind and thoughtful.

The first morning I walked onto the unit, I felt like a new kid at school. I needed every ounce of God's promised strength to keep me there. But he answered my prayers, and those of the many who had been praying for me. Although it was tough, and there were no few tears shed in the quiet sanctuary of the staff toilets from time to time, I miraculously made it through the day.

A few weeks passed.

Then, one morning, as I went on duty, the Sister called me to one side before we went into our early morning handover meeting. She asked me if I felt up to doing an actual delivery. I was lost for words—a very unusual occurrence for me! I stammered, 'Who, me?' She smiled encouragingly, 'Yes, you. We are going to be really busy. The student midwives can provide much of the cover in the ante- and post-natal wards. I am really going to need you in the labour ward today.'

I knew, despite my apprehensions, that it was time, and that it would have been unreasonable of me to refuse this very reasonable request—even though everything in me wanted to run home and curl up in my bed with the covers over my head. The Sister had been more than patient with me over the past few weeks; watching out for me, and protecting me whenever it was possible.

Now it was time to prove, both to myself and to everyone else, that I really did believe that God's promise of

His all-surpassing power could enable me to do this.

Entering the labour ward, I found myself in the presence of a young mum and her equally young husband. They both looked terrified. I introduced myself and chatted with them for a while, trying to put them at their ease.

The young woman's name was Tracy. Her husband was James. Tracy had been in labour for around four hours and everything was going really well, both for her and her baby. Despite this, over the next few hours, as her labour progressed, she became more and more anxious. James went off to get a coffee, and I sat with Tracy. In between her contractions, we chatted.

Tracy opened up to me, explaining that it wasn't the contractions that were making her anxious, but the fact that her youngest sister, Sarah Jane, had been born with complicated cerebral palsy, and had been poorly from birth. Her long-term diagnosis was very poor as she suffered with severe grand mal fits. Lately, she seemed to be deteriorating rapidly. Her spine had become more and more twisted from scoliosis and she needed constant care.

Then Tracy smiled, and added, 'But she's also wonderful. She's so full of courage. When she isn't fitting, her personality and sense of humour shine through her eyes, and we know that she's still in there somewhere.'

Tracy confided how there had been particular complications during her Mum's labour which had resulted in Sarah Jane's condition. Although she knew that her own labour was going well, she was terrified that something might go wrong that would affect her baby. She felt that she wouldn't be able to cope in the way that her Mum had.

My heart went out to her, and, suddenly, my own anxieties became secondary. As we chatted, I did all that I could to reassure her. On James' return, I left them for a few minutes. I went into the little room next door, where I prayed for them. I remembered how so many people had faithfully prayed for me the night I was in labour, and how those prayers had held me in a way that nothing else could.

Two hours later, I delivered their baby, and introduced Tracy and James to their beautiful baby girl. Laying her on her Mummy's chest, I realised that my heart was not full of pain, as I had feared that it might be. Rather, I was overwhelmed by a feeling of immense joy. And a wonderful sense of privilege that I had been given the opportunity to be a tiny part of this miracle.

Tracy and James called their little girl Jane, after Tracy's sister. I thought that was precious. As I watched them both holding their perfect little girl, I prayed that Tracy's sister might live long enough to get to know her little niece.

Then I quietly slipped out of the room, found a quiet place, and wept.

I was reminded of Sarah Jane's story some years later, while working at the Children's Hospice in Cambridge. One of the nurses there, Hilary, wrote a beautiful poem for a child that she had supported for some years. The words highlight the right perspective to have when looking at people, seeing not merely what is on the outside, but what is on the inside.

Just as Tracy had described her sister to me.

Look down on twisted beauty, and pity if you must.
Look down on senseless suffering, on wasted life and love.
But if you do, you haven't known, you haven't come to share
Those moments caught in just a glimpse, captured in light and
*   air.*
There's nothing here to taint with greed, with selfishness, or
*   pride.*
No jealousy, contempt or scorn, no treachery to hide.
Look up to strength and beauty, to courage, and joy of living.
Look deep into those wondrous eyes, see dignity, and giving.
Look at her hands, expressing trust, her hair cascading
*   laughter.*
And sense the tireless, endless love that follows her long after.

It leaves that outward twisted shell, and hears the voice inside
  you tell:
I know, I sense, I care, and I love.
I've played my part,
I've left my heart.

(Hilary Rickards)

If we are honest, we are all capable of making snap judgments when people do not measure up to certain expectations. Sadly, we live today in a society that is so focused on the outward appearance.

Aways looking for perfection.

So obsessed with celebrity image that other things, far more beautiful and precious, can be lost.

Over the years, I have seen so many children and young people who don't measure up in the eyes of our 'perfect' society. But if we open our eyes, and look beyond the outward shell, there we will find treasures in abundance.

In 1 Samuel 16 we read the story of David, who was chosen over his brothers—seven in all—to be king. The Lord instructed Samuel, when he went to Jesse, David's father, to choose a king, not to consider height, or appearance, for the Lord does not look at the outward appearance, but the on the heart (v.7).

Had it been me, I may well have considered that David had little to commend him, compared to his brothers, and chosen quite differently.

But God knew what He was looking for.

And so He does with us.

I remember one year at Spring Harvest hearing Joni Eareckson Tada speaking about her life and her experiences. She declared her conviction that she had been able to share God's love from sitting in a wheelchair in ways that she could never have done had she still been able to walk.

How amazing, I thought, to only be able to move your head, and yet to be able to say that.

As she continued, I could see why.

Despite the restriction of not being able to move her arms or legs, she could still speak of God's love, as well as help others in similar circumstances through her extensive and multi-faceted work with JAF Ministries.

I was aware of something of her richly diverse ministry. How she used her wonderful voice to sing God's praises and had recorded numerous albums. She had also authored more than twenty books. Remarkably, she had learned to paint inspiring and beautiful pictures, using her mouth.

For all these accomplishments and achievements, as I observed her, most striking of all was the beauty that shone out of her. It was a beauty that no amount of makeup, or expensive designer clothes, could give.

Her beauty came from the soul.

I have sat with so many parents whose children had the most debilitating of illnesses and disabilities. Yet, without fail, they would affirm that their children, with all of their limitations, had given them a gift of such richness and beauty that could never be measured or quantified.

God never writes us off.

Thank God that he doesn't judge us as we sometimes would judge others, but loves us and uses us, despite our outward circumstances, for His eternal glory.

During the next six months, it was quite remarkable to me that two mums were transferred to our unit after having stillborn babies. In both cases, their child's diagnosis was anencephaly. According to the Sister on the unit, as far as she could recall, no mother had either been delivered or transferred there with this diagnosis for over two years.

On both occasions, I was on duty when they were admitted. And I knew this was no coincidence.

The evening before the first lady was to be admitted, my sister's words came back to me, clear and strong. 'What if this is God's time, and the right timing for this particular job, and you miss it? It would be a shame to look back with regrets.'

I had asked Bernie, 'Do you believe that such sadness can be overcome, eventually, and the experience used to help others?' Her reply had been that God doesn't waste even our most painful experiences, but it takes both courage and faith to let Him use them.

I knew that she was right.

But was it too soon?

Would I be strong enough to offer this level of support?

That night, I looked in my Bible for the reading she had given me and read again from Hebrews 12,

> *'No discipline seems pleasant at the time, but painful. Later on, however, it produces a harvest of righteousness and peace for those who have been trained by it. Therefore, strengthen your feeble arms and weak knees. "Make level paths for your feet," so that the lame may not be disabled, but rather healed.'* (vv. 11-13).

I did not of course disclose my own experience to either of the mums, in the same way that Bernie had not with me. I knew that I could pray for them, however, and support them, and somehow touch their pain because of my own.

God gave me the words, and an understanding, that I know I could never have offered had my baby not been born with this same condition. It is hard to explain. But that is the way it was. A common tragedy, a common bond.

During the following weeks and months, the Lord gave me many opportunities to support mums who were struggling with loss or disappointment in one way or another.

I myself had suffered an early miscarriage, just six months after we were married, whilst living in France. We were away from family and friends, and felt somewhat isolated as we struggled with the loss of our baby, at just eight weeks' gestation.

The doctor suggested to us that we should get on with life and try again, pointing out that it was not unusual to suffer a miscarriage during a first pregnancy. His hope was that next time all would be well.

We wept, and coped with the disappointment and sadness very much on our own. I had now come to realise, however, while supporting other mums on the maternity unit, that miscarriage, although different from my experience of having a stillborn baby, is in many ways no less painful.

Death is still death.

Whenever, and however, it occurs, it is worthy of respect and grief.

I am so thankful that today miscarriage is regarded with much more sympathy and understanding, and that support is offered, and the opportunity to grieve encouraged, in a much more significant way than was the case when I had mine.

I thanked God for showing me then, what I had not understood previously.

I was very aware that I had been in the right place at the right time, able to offer help and support to those mums, not because there was anything special about me. Rather, this was God's first step in teaching me that my daughter's life, and her premature death, could touch the hearts of others in ways I had not previously understood.

16

BEN

The next five months passed by with a quiet acceptance of all that had gone before.

I thought about our baby every day.

When the pain caused by the memory of the day that we had lost her became too hard to bear, I would let it linger in my mind for one moment longer, knowing that if I could survive those feelings, and they did not overwhelm or destroy me, there was hope for the future.

It was eight months almost to the day that our baby had died. I was on my way to work. It was early October, and the leaves on the trees were beginning to change colour. It was a lovely time of year as the leaves turned from green to beautiful shades of gold, russet, and red. Later, they would fall to the ground where they would lie, a carpet beautifully laid by nature itself.

When Chris and I lived in France, in a small town on the River Loire, we used to take prayer walks by the river. The riverside was lined with trees. In the autumn, we would feel the leaves crunching under our feet as we walked. This replenishing of nature time and time again is a graphic reminder that there is a season for everything. A reminder that, as Christians, our times are in his hands.

I found comfort in reflecting on these things, and the words of Scripture came to mind:

There is a time for everything,
and a season for every activity under the heavens:
a time to be born and a time to die,
a time to plant and a time to uproot,

a time to kill and a time to heal,
a time to tear down and a time to build,
a time to weep and a time to laugh,
a time to mourn and a time to dance,
a time to scatter stones and a time to gather them,
a time to embrace and a time to refrain,
a time to search and a time to give up,
a time to keep and a time to throw away,
a time to tear and a time to mend,
a time to be silent and a time to speak,
a time to love and a time to hate,
a time for war and a time for peace.

(Ecclesiastes 3:1-8)

On my way to work, I got out of the car to post some mail. Suddenly, a feeling of nausea swept over me. I had had a few hectic days, and knew that I was over-tired. Life was busy on the whole, and for that I was glad.

Less time to think.

Katie was our little bundle of joy, and there was not a single day that passed when I did not thank God for her being in our lives. Now over two years old, she was full of life and energy.

Life at our church was full, with all of its different activities. Chris and I ran the children's work together, which was fun. On those Tuesdays, Mum would look after Katie for us in the afternoons and evenings—something that, to this day, Katie treasures the memories of.

There were outings, walks to the beach, picnics in the garden. Or, sometimes, if it was raining, the picnic would be transferred to the lounge, where Mum would lay out a table-cloth on the carpet, with all the food spread out. Of course, all of Katie's stuffed animals and dolls were invited.

As I highlighted at the beginning of this book, memories are so very special. And Katie was just at the beginning of creating her own memory-store of treasures, just as I had as a child.

We were busy on the unit that day. Gradually, the feeling of nausea passed. Nevertheless, after feeling the same over the next few mornings, I finally began to admit to myself that this was probably more than just tiredness. My monthly periods had been unusually irregular since I had lost the baby. I wasn't too worried, and put it down to my hormones settling down again.

But now I began seriously thinking about the real possibility of actually being pregnant. I was filled with a mixture of emotions, fluctuating between abject fear and absolute joy.

There was a time for everything.

Perhaps this was the time for us, when new life had begun.

One afternoon I decided to take Katie for a walk. We wrapped up warmly and, as she skipped along and chattered away beside me, I looked down at her. She grinned up at me and pleaded, 'Come on, Mummy. Skip with me.' At that moment, I knew with all of my heart I wanted to be pregnant again. To experience those wonderful moments. Of course, they wouldn't be in exactly the same way. But wonderful none the less.

Another child would be such a blessing.

Such a gift.

I determined that I wouldn't say anything to Chris until I was absolutely sure, as I felt it wouldn't be fair. However, later that day, once Katie was in bed, I just couldn't stop myself. The possibility of this particular miracle just had to be shared with him straight away. The words came tumbling out of my mouth. They were peppered, of course, with 'It may not be.' 'It's very early days.' 'If it is, we mustn't get our hopes up, must we?'

I remember Chris just smiling at me in his teasing sort of way.

'What is it?' I enquired.

'You have your smile back,' he replied.

If all went well with this pregnancy, I knew that in just eight short months or so we could be holding our new-born in our arms. I also knew that our little baby girl would never be forgotten.

For she was born.

And she would always be loved, her memory forever alive in our hearts.

Our Children

Ours are the silent ones,
Ours are the unseen ones,
Whose memory will lie forever in our hearts;
Whose memory will also carry anguish.
Our arms are empty,
Our hearts are full,
For our children, though still and silent,
In untimely death, are real people.
Named as all children are named,
Loved as all children are loved,
Dreamed for as all children are dreamed for.
Planning for a future as parents do,
We perceive the bud, but are denied its blossom.
Our children are the silent ones,
Our children are the unseen ones.
Within our hearts they are loved and mourned.
Time lays upon our hearts to heal,
But memory gives us quiet joy,
For our children, born and loved eternally.

(Source unknown)

Within the next four weeks, the doctor had pronounced the wonderful news that I was in fact pregnant again. The due date was the end of June, just seven short months away.

As I walked away from the doctor's surgery, I could not

have been more thankful.

We decided at first that we would wait until after twelve weeks before sharing the news with others. Then we reflected, why wait? We needed the prayers and support of all those who loved us. So we announced our joyful news. Everyone was overjoyed, and we felt held by the multitude of their good wishes and prayers.

In view of our previous loss, an appointment was made to see a consultant at the Bristol Royal Infirmary. Walking into the building, a feeling of sadness washed over me. It was the first time we had been back there since our little one had died.

I wondered what would be our experience this time, as we walked into the consultant's office. He congratulated us warmly on our news, then proceeded to recommend that because of my previous history it would be preferable for the baby to be born at that hospital. He also reminded us that there was a one-in-twenty chance of having another child with anencephaly.

Hearing this again for the first time since that awful day brought painful and unwelcome memories flooding back.

The consultant advised us that he did have some concerns. He added, however, that there were tests that could be carried out to detect any possible abnormalities. He strongly advised us to have these tests carried out since we would certainly not want to repeat our previous difficult journey, simply to find ourselves, at its end, living with the same tragic outcome.

The consultant explained that I could have an amniocentesis: a procedure that involved removing a small amount of fluid from around the amniotic sack. He warned us that there was a small chance that this could trigger a miscarriage, but that this was the only way of testing for this condition. We thanked the consultant, advising him that we would go away and carefully consider the information and advice he had given us.

All the way home from the hospital, we reflected on what we had heard.

My previously happy mood had been somewhat dampened by the events of the day. We were grateful for the consultant's advice. To have to go through the trauma of another possible stillbirth seemed unthinkable. However, if we went ahead with the amniocentesis, there was a slight risk of triggering a miscarriage.

Moreover, were we to opt for this procedure, in the event that the outcome of the test was negative, we would be offered a termination of the pregnancy. There was no other option. Nothing else to be done. We both knew that, for us, this was simply not an option. So there was no point in putting our baby at risk by undergoing the amniocentesis.

In many respects, it was a frightening decision to make. We believed it to be the right one, however. If the worst should happen again, God would give us the strength to bear it.

It was now not in our hands, but His.

The next weeks passed quickly. Other than some morning sickness, I felt well. Before we knew it, it was Christmas-time again. Had she lived, our little girl would have been ten months old and about to experience her first Christmas.

I began to imagine her in my mind's eye. I smiled to myself at the thought of her crawling around by now, reaching into the boxes of ornaments, playing with the tinsel, and being encouraged into mischief by her sister— though too young to have any real understanding of the joys of Christmas, of course.

'Next year, though,' I thought, 'things will be different. And then she'll really catch the excitement of it all.'

Suddenly, I realised that I had been lost deep in my own thoughts. There would be no next year for her. For one fleeting moment, I had forgotten. As I rested my hand on my tummy, and thought about the new life inside me, I was thankful.

But an overwhelming sadness also swept over me as I was brutally reminded that she would never experience such joys with our family, or our family with her. Moments such as those were difficult to cope with. They left me feeling unsettled, full of emotions that I couldn't truly understand, or explain, even to myself, let alone to any one else.

So I kept them hidden, imagining it to be just grief.

According to the Bible, 'There is a time to grieve, and a time to dance.' I was far from dancing. This was something I had to go through. One day it would be better, I repeatedly told myself. I was nevertheless left with a feeling of such utter and complete emptiness that at times I wondered, 'Could even this most precious, and wanted, child growing inside me fill such a void?'

In my pain, I began to doubt even that.

This was our first Christmas without the baby we had expected to be with us. Whilst the fun and festivities went ahead, which was important for us all, it was different.

In his book *The Lion, the Witch, and the Wardrobe* C. S. Lewis presents the land of Narnia. Before the return of Aslan, the king, it is observed of Narnia that it was always winter, but never Christmas. I realised that that was exactly how I had been feeling. As I wrote earlier, Christmas had always been for me a precious time of year, full of warmth and joy. Yet this one simply felt like a never-ending winter, without any of the joys of that particular season.

Along with this feeling was a deep-seated concern for the safety of the baby I was now carrying.

Did it suffer from the same condition as our little girl?

Would there be any other problems?

How would I cope with giving birth, after my last awful experience?

How would I survive the next six months without knowing?

So many questions, with no answers to offer me the

much-needed peace that I desired.

Around that time, I was reading the account of Noah and the building of the ark, in the book of Genesis. It struck me afresh how Noah had trusted God under the strangest of circumstances. What faith it took to build an ark of such a size, to look such a fool in the eyes of those around him, watching and mocking him. After all, where was the water?

Then, every living thing upon the face of the earth not sheltered within the ark was wiped out by the flood. And Noah was waiting for God's next move—which I am sure was a lot harder that it sounds. In chapter eight, verse one of the book of Genesis, we read that God remembered Noah.

He had trusted his God against all the odds.

And God had not forgotten him.

Later on in the narrative we read that God blessed Noah. He gave him a promise that never again would all life be cut off by the waters of a flood. Never again would there be a flood to destroy the earth. And God set His rainbow in the sky as a sign of the promise between them.

As I read those words at that particular time, I was filled with a sense of new hope. If God could do such a thing, make such a promise, He could take control of this situation for me right here and now. Suddenly, I felt fresh hope for this baby, that all would be well. That this would not happen to us again.

Of course, I couldn't know for sure. Even so, I now found myself facing the following six months with a renewed sense of peace. Whatever happened next, I knew that God would somehow surround me with an ark: a safe place to wait until, like Noah, I could safely step out onto secure ground.

Just after New Year, Katie and I had a free afternoon, and we decided to visit my sister, who lived in the next village. It was a lovely day. Sunny, but chilly. After a chat and a cup of tea, we decided to go for a walk down the country road to the village shops.

The children had not yet gone back to school so we were joined by Katie's three young cousins. We bought some sweets at one of the little shops. This took quite a while as the children deliberated over what they wanted, changing their minds several times before actually deciding, as children do. While we were in the shop, we could hear a noise on the roof. Realising that it had started to rain, we browsed for a little longer, and chatted to the shopkeeper.

Once the rain had stopped, we headed for home. It was lovely as we walked out onto the pavement. The sun had come out after the shower, and it was warm on our faces. As we strolled back up the road, Matthew, the only boy, decided to jump in as many puddles as he could find, accompanied by the screams of his sisters, and Katie.

As we passed by a field, my sister stopped suddenly, exclaiming, 'Just look at that! Isn't it beautiful?' I leaned on the fence to look. Suddenly, I had tears pouring down my cheeks. There it was. The most beautiful rainbow, stretching in all its colourful glory across the sky. Sue put her arm around me, enquiring, 'Whatever is it? What's wrong?'

'I don't really know,' I replied, 'but I suddenly feel that it's safe to step out of the ark.'

While we walked home, I filled her in on my Noah experience.

For the first time since the beginning of this pregnancy, I felt that I was standing on safe and firm ground. During the next six months, I allowed myself to feel the joy of the possibilities to come. I was determined now not to let myself look back on this time as one filled with anxieties. I would not rob Chris and Katie of this unique blessing. One which could never be revisited.

I also wanted our baby to feel a sense of calm and well-being while it was growing inside me. And so, although I didn't for one moment forget about our baby girl, when anxieties rose to the surface, I asked God to give me a sense of His peace and love, enabling me to cope.

When the hospital offered me a scan at twenty-two weeks, because of my past history, I was keen to have it. Once again, our church prayed for us when we went for the appointment.

It felt almost surreal as I went though the same procedure as before. Chris came in with me this time, and I cannot put into words the utter relief and overwhelming joy we experienced when we were given the news that all was well. There were no indications of any abnormalities.

When we broke this wonderful news to family and friends it was received with whoops of joy and thankfulness. We walked out into the garden when we got home, where we prayed, weeping tears of gratitude through our prayer of thanksgiving.

> *Through the wetness of your tears,*
> *Your own sorrow will begin to glisten.*
> *You can go from the pits, where it is black,*
> *To beige, and then to rainbows, which come from tears in our lives.*
> *Your constant habit of being a joy collector will be your therapy.*

(Barbara Johnson, *Love Leaps*)

The anniversary of our daughter's death was on February 6th.

We had some lovely cards from family and friends, whose thoughts and prayers were with us. The cards took us both by surprise. It would have been her first birthday, had she lived, and everything would have been so different.

We were so grateful that she hadn't been forgotten, and we were touched by people's kindness to us. The day itself came and went quietly. Chris and I were both lost in our own thoughts.

We had no memories of her.

No life to reflect upon.

There were no sweet or funny stories to share, as you do over a life lived.

There were no photo albums to browse through and smile at.

There was only sadness and pain.

It was then, for the first time, that I was overwhelmed with a deep sense of regret. Not simply about the fact that she had died, but that we had not given her a place in our lives to live, to be remembered.

I quickly pushed the thoughts to the back of my mind. Don't go there. If you do, I urged myself, you will not survive.

So that is where those thoughts remained.

They rose to the surface from time to time, only to be pushed back again and again. Not until five years later was I to face those regrets head on.

I was still working part-time, right up to the end of May. I was now really looking forward to giving up work and becoming a full-time mum again for a while. The last few weeks were spent making sure everything was ready. As we didn't know whether our baby was a boy or a girl—as was the way in those days—we had decided to use the things that we had bought for our little girl, as most of them were white anyway.

It comforted us to think that she would have liked that. Afterwards, once the baby had arrived and we knew its gender, we could shop for pinks or blues.

At thirty-nine weeks, I was waddling around and counting the days. I was experiencing Braxton Hicks contractions and kept wondering, Is this it?

But nothing happened.

At around four o'clock on the afternoon of June 25th, I had just started to organise tea for Katie when my friend Carol phoned to see how I was. We were chatting away when suddenly my waters broke. For some reason, I didn't tell her what had happened. Perhaps I wanted Chris to know this exciting news first. I calmly uttered, 'Well I'd better be off now, as I need to get tea sorted.'

Chris was in his study, and I called him. His face was a picture as I stood smiling in a tiny puddle of water.

We rang the hospital and were advised to come straight in. Clearly, they weren't taking any chances with this baby. We called my parents who came straight over to collect Katie. She was two years and ten months old by then, and the absolute joy of our hearts. We had explained to her that Mummy was going into hospital to have her little brother or sister, and that she would be staying with her Nan and Pop.

As Mum and Dad went upstairs to get her toys, she looked up at me with big eyes and enquired, 'Will the baby be coming home this time, Mummy?' Perhaps it showed a lack of faith on my part, but I didn't know how to answer her.

I desperately wanted to respond, 'Yes, yes, the baby will be coming home, darling.'

But the words stuck in my throat.

Chris didn't hear the question, as he was collecting her things to put into Dad's car. But at that moment he picked her up. 'Come on, Daisy. Kiss Mummy goodbye, and let's get you into Pop's car.'

'OK, Daddy.'

She gave me a big hug and a kiss, and the moment had passed. How good the Lord is at both understanding our needs, and meeting them.

At around six o'clock we arrived at the hospital. My contractions had already started and labour progressed well without any problems. I walked around my room as much as possible, since lying on the bed was so uncomfortable.

It was Wimbledon fortnight, and they were still playing into the evening. The room had a small television, and we both loved the tennis. So, for a time, it was a distraction for both of us. After a while, however, I couldn't really have cared who was winning. I was more interested in where the gas and air was!

There was a rocking chair in the room, which I made use

of. It reminded me of the times I had sat in my chair at home, sobbing, and feeling a sense of foreboding about my last pregnancy.

This was different. For, as far as we knew, this baby was all right. When my tummy turned over and the butterflies began, and I could feel the worries creeping in, I remembered the rainbow and God's promise of assurance to Noah. Since that day, I had felt that I had been standing on more solid ground, and that what had happened before would not now happen to us again.

However, after ten hours in labour, the next phase was hard—emotionally more than physically. All the memories of last time came flooding back, and I now desperately needed it to be over.

To see my child.

To hold it, and know that it was whole and safe.

Doubts began to creep in, and I was filled with guilt over that. After all, God had been so faithful in all his dealings with me. I now felt such a failure for not trusting Him more.

With every pain I knew that I was starting to panic. The midwife kept encouraging, 'Come on. You're OK. You're an old hand at this. You've done it before.' She didn't seem to have taken on board what before actually meant to me. Not even Chris's gentleness could take away the sense of panic that was rising within me. I felt the peace that I had previously been experiencing slipping away, and feared that I was somehow slipping out of His grasp.

I was suddenly very afraid.

Chris asked me if I wanted him to read from the Gideon Bible that was on my locker. I nodded, though I knew that I probably couldn't concentrate, since the pains were now coming thick and fast. He sat beside me, held my hand, and began reading from Psalm 139.

'You have searched me, LORD, and you know me. You know when I sit and when I rise; you perceive my thoughts from

afar. You discern my going out and my lying down; you are familiar with all my ways. Before a word is on my tongue you, LORD, know it completely. You hem me in behind and before, and you lay your hand upon me. Such knowledge is too wonderful for me, too lofty for me to attain. Where can I go from your Spirit? Where can I flee from your presence? If I go up to the heavens, you are there; if I make my bed in the depths, you are there. If I rise on the wings of the dawn, if I settle on the far side of the sea, even there your hand will guide me, your right hand will hold me fast.'

(Psalm 139:1–10)

As Chris read those words, I was struck once again by the truth that God knew me so very well, and was indeed holding me fast. I could not hide my thoughts, or my fears from Him. And He would not hide Himself from me. This really was about my relationship with God To know that He understood me so very well, and loved me still.

To be reminded of that at such a time as this was—had to be—from Him. As He held onto me with His firm hand, so I clung to Him. And knew that wherever I was, He was there, and would remain so.

There had been times over the past seventeen months when I had felt quite lost, and that no one, not even God, was able to find me. So I cried out to Him again to find the thing that was lost—in this case me—and to carry me to a safe and secure place.

Within the next half an hour, our beautiful son Ben was born. He weighed just five pounds and ten ounces. We were left in no doubt that there was absolutely nothing wrong with his lungs as he made his presence felt in the world. And, I might add, has continued to do so, in his own most precious and unique kind of way.

As I held him, I wept tears of joy. Chris held my hand, and I watched him stroke his little boy's cheek. There was nothing to be said; nothing to be done. There was just our hearts united, lifted up to God with such a depth of gratitude, that no words were needed. In fact, they would have been superfluous on this occasion. They could never have explained, or added to, that particular wonderful moment.

Later, when I had had a wash and enjoyed a much-needed cup of tea, I just lay holding Ben: smelling him, and loving him. This was a moment, just seventeen months before, that I had been robbed of.

Ben had not been born simply to replace that which we had so cruelly lost. But God had been faithful. Despite my fears and doubts, at times, He had not given up on me. By giving us Ben, He was doing a new thing in our lives, offering us different joys and blessings to the ones we had perhaps expected. It was His faithfulness and persistence that had brought us to this place.

To this day, I can feel the emotion of that moment while holding Ben. The feeling was almost palpable. It was a moment I have never forgotten, and will never forget.

Some years ago, my now six-foot plus nephew Matt—the one who loved jumping in the puddles—had been given his dad's wedding ring by his mum. His dad, my sister Sue's husband, Les, sadly and tragically died at the age of forty-three. Les was the loveliest of men: a gentle giant. Everybody loved him. He was just that sort of guy.

When he died, it left us all heartbroken.

Matt was thrilled to have his dad's wedding ring and wore it all the time. One day, he went to Cheddar, which was near where he lived. There was a reservoir there, and on summer evenings Matt sometimes used to visit it with his friends.

On this occasion, he was there with three of his friends, and he began throwing stones, skimming them across the water. It was about half an hour before dusk. As he picked up another stone, he heard a clang, and realised, to his horror, that his dad's wedding ring had slipped off his finger and dropped into the water.

He immediately went to the edge of the water and, much to his relief, could see the ring a few feet in. He waded in, only to find that it was an old coin. He stayed looking into the water until it was dark, but gradually realised that no amount of searching was going to find the precious ring.

Matt wrote a letter to his mum, explaining to her what had happened. He just couldn't face informing her that he had lost something so precious to her—even more precious to her, in a way, than it was to him. Although deep down he knew that she would be more concerned for his feelings than the lost ring, it was little comfort.

The following day, Matt took an extended lunch break from work, and went back to the reservoir, spending an hour searching for the ring.

It was nowhere to be found.

For four weeks he continued to visit the reservoir, sometimes two or three times a week. Gradually, hope began to fade that he would ever find it. Yet he was reluctant to give up. His mum knew that he had been going back to search for the ring, and was still very upset over its loss.

One evening, she sat him down and explained that, although she fully understood how upset he was, she did not want him to be so consumed by this, and it was time to let go. She knew that was how his dad would feel about it, too.

Nonetheless, one day, straight after work, Matt decided to go back and look again. It was a lovely sunny evening, and the water level had been dropping considerably due to the dry weather. Matt suddenly noticed that about ten feet from the water's edge there was a glinting object. He took his shoes off and waded into the water.

When he stood over the object, he could see that it was the ring. He remarked later that he didn't have the words to describe how he felt at that moment. Knowing that he had found the ring, all he wanted to do was tell his mum, and then everyone else.

Over four weeks after losing the ring, Matt had found it

again. From the initial time it was lost it must have travelled around twenty-five to thirty feet into the depths of the water. Later that day, Matt again put pen to paper, and this is what he wrote to his mum.

Dear Mum,
Please read the note first and then open the envelope.
One day a young man lost something very precious to him. Several weeks later, something amazing happened. He found the thing, which was lost.

When Matt's mum opened the envelope, there was the ring!

I found Matt's story so inspiring that I asked if I could include it here. Matt never gave up looking for the ring. He knew that another could never replace it, and, in this case, his own faithfulness and persistence had paid off.

And so I have come to learn over the years that God never lets us go; never loses sight of us. When we stand alone, feeling lost and afraid, He will come and find us, never giving up, always searching; waiting for us simply to be found by Him again.

He had taught me so many lessons during the past two years.

Little did I know that there was still much to be learned in the months and years ahead.

17

MY CUP OVERFLOWS

Chris had the happy task of phoning our family and friends to spread the wonderful news that all was well. Ben Jack had arrived, safe and sound.

The following day, I was sent back to Weston-super-Mare, to our local postnatal unit, Ashcombe House. It was a lovely old house that had been converted into a maternity unit. It was set in beautiful grounds where literally dozens of squirrels could be seen scampering around, darting up and down trees as if their lives depended on it. A happy place to reside, indeed.

My cup was full and overflowing.

The staff were really lovely, and I enjoyed my stay. Those few special days spent getting to know my little boy were precious to me. We had a stream of visits from family and friends, and I reflected on how different it all was this time around.

The first time Katie came to visit, her face was a picture as she stared into the perspex-sided crib that Ben was lying in. She tapped on the side of the crib and, looking up, asked, 'Can I hold him, Mummy?' She sat on the bed. As I lifted Ben out and let her hold him, she just giggled.

When she enquired, 'Is he coming home with us, Mummy?' my eyes filled with tears at her innocent question. I replied, with utter joy, 'Yes, darling. He most certainly is coming home with us.' 'Oh, good!' she exclaimed. 'I can play with him, then.'

Ben was so tiny that even the smallest baby-grows were too big for him. My Mum and sister managed to find him a special make of very tiny baby clothes called Dolly Mixture.

They were so cute.

When Katie saw them, she laughed, and asked if, when Ben was too big for them, she could have them to put on her dolly. And that's exactly what she did. She still has her tiny-tears doll to this day.

And, yes, it is still dressed in Ben's tiny baby-grow.

The day Chris and Katie came to collect me, and Ben, I was so excited as I waited in the day room for them to arrive. I remember that it was a gloriously sunny day. When we got home, I felt so thankful. Ben and I had both survived the journey of his birth, and life now lay before us with all of the expectations and possibilities of joys to come.

For the first time in a long time, I was filled with a sweet contentment that perhaps only a new mum can fully comprehend.

The following days were met with new joy as we all got to know Ben. He was a happy baby, and within six weeks was sleeping right through the night.

Katie loved him.

On her third birthday, she insisted on showing her little brother off to her friends as they came to her birthday party. 'This is my new baby brother.' she would say, proudly adding, 'And I help Mummy take care of him.'

It was the start of a special friendship between them that has lasted over the years. Of course, they have had their moments, as siblings do. Nonetheless, underneath there has always been a deep friendship and loyalty to each other that has remained rock solid to this day.

I was very protective of Ben, at first. The second child in a family is often treated in a more relaxed way than the first. Having lost a daughter, however, made this feel like the first time all over again for me. I found myself worrying unnecessarily at times over every little thing. This was neither healthy nor helpful for either of us.

As Ben grew from baby to toddler, I had to learn afresh that there are two things that we can give to our children.

One is roots. The other is wings. I was rediscovering that the former is easier to give than the latter.

As Barbara Johnson writes in her little book, *Love Leaps*,

> *We have to give our children to God and then take our hands off. It is like wrapping a package up and putting on a label, and then being able to send it, without our special directions of where to go, but letting God put the address on the label or on that life.'*

Weeks rolled into months, and then years, and we had so much to be thankful for.

Although Ben suffered from asthma in his early years, several times ending up being hospitalised, we were always fortunate to have a brilliant doctor and excellent hospital on hand. We felt very supported by them.

Ben always amazed us at his quiet acceptance of his condition. When at times he lay on the sofa, pale and gasping for air, yet uncomplaining, it was so heart-breaking to see. He regularly had to go for hospital checks, and had numerous blood tests done—especially during the first six years of his life—but God had given him, it seemed, an easy-going and uncomplaining nature that helped him to accept his lot, even at that young age.

We had one further year in Weston-super-Mare following Ben's arrival. It was precious having my family close by during that time. Ben was just over a year old, and Katie was four, when we moved to Birmingham, where Chris had accepted the call to be the Minister of the Medical Mission, an independent evangelical church.

It was a church I already knew, since I had attended there whilst undergoing my midwifery training. Yet I struggled with the thought of moving, at first. Leaving my family was a big issue, as was leaving a church that had been so supportive through the most tragic time in our lives so far.

They had helped to bring light into a dark time in our

lives, and I felt vulnerable to be leaving that support behind. It was also hard to leave our relatively small, and very rural, seaside town, where the countryside beckoned, and the beach and sea reminded me of wonderful childhood days.

Returning to the big city was a challenge. Although I had loved it when I had been there previously, whilst independent and single, returning now with two small children seemed a different prospect altogether.

One evening, while still at our church in Weston, we were having a Bible study and prayer meeting. I felt that it was right to share honestly something of my concerns with the people there. I knew that they would pray for me. As I began to speak, the tears flowed, and I realised how big a struggle this had become for me.

The following day, during my daily time with the Lord, I was reading from the well-known devotional book that I used at the time, *Streams in the Desert*. I was pleading with the Lord for clear confirmation that this move was indeed right for us as a family.

I had always said to Chris that I would go anywhere the Lord asked us to go, but I had to be sure that it was He who was sending us. As long as I was certain of being in His will, I knew, whatever life threw at us, that we could depend on Him to help us to cope, since He Himself had brought us to that place. My reading that day included a poem.

Let me walk in the fields

I said: 'Let me walk in the field;'
God said: 'No walk in the town;'
I said: 'There are no flowers there;'
He said: 'No flowers, but a crown.'

I said: 'But the sky is black.
There is nothing but noise and din;'
But He wept as He sent me back,
'There is more,' He said: 'There is sin.'

I said: 'But the air is thick,
And fogs are veiling the sun;'
He answered: 'Yet souls are sick,
And souls in the dark undone.'

I said: 'I shall miss the light,
And friends will miss me, they say;'
He answered me, 'Choose tonight,
If I am to miss you, or they.'

I pleaded for time to be given;
He said: 'Is it hard to decide?
It will not seem so hard in Heaven
To have followed the steps of your guide.'

I cast one look at the fields,
Then set my face to the town;
He said: 'My child, do you yield?
Will you leave the flowers for the crown?'

Then into His hand went mine,
And into my heart came He;
And I walked in a path divine,
The path I had feared to see.

The next Sunday, I was able to give testimony to God's goodness and the absolute peace that I had experienced since reading those words on that day.

On our final Sunday in Weston we had a thanksgiving service, and a wonderful tea was provided for us. There were cards, gifts, flowers, and lots of tears to send us on our way. The most precious thing I was given that day was from one of our young people, Lorraine.

She had had the words from the poem that God had given me copied, and had collected wild flowers, which she had dried and pressed, laying them around the edge of the poem. She had then had the whole montage put into a pretty frame. On it, she had put a little card. The words read, 'To Babs. So that you will never forget.'

I still have that poem and have often read it when facing times of uncertainty, thanking God for Lorraine and her gift, which, as far as I am concerned, just went on giving.

Within the first few weeks of being at our new church— the Mission, as it was commonly known—and even before Chris's official induction, my faith in God's leading was challenged. I collapsed and was taken into hospital.

The diagnosis was meningitis.

How thankful I was for the reassurance that God had already given me: the reassurance that, whatever happened, we were in the right place, at the right time.

He would take care of us.

While we were at the Mission, Katie experienced school for the first time. Happily, she loved it. Ben took his first wobbly steps, and began to talk. He has never stopped since. Sorry, Ben, but it's true.

I already had friends at the church, my friend Carol, whom you met earlier in this story, being one of them. We were to make many more over the next two years. And we would see God touch lives in some very special ways during our time there.

Just over two years later, we moved to Northwood, in Middlesex, where Chris returned to being a full-time student, studying for a Master's degree in biblical interpretation at London Bible College (now London School of Theology).

We rented a lovely house and settled into our new life. Katie settled into a good school, soon making lots of friends. Ben started play school. Despite still struggling with his asthma, he always met life head on.

Our year at LBC was precious. We made many lovely friendships, some of which still continue today. We attended an extremely welcoming and friendly church, with wonderful ministry and worship, which blessed us all as a family. I got involved in the Mums and Toddlers group.

All in all, life was sweet.

Most of all, Chris and I both felt so utterly blessed to have our precious daughter, and son.

We had so much to be grateful for.

Why was it, then, that, almost four years after the death of our baby, I still quietly wept at night?

No one—not even Chris—was aware of how I felt, of my on-going sadness and struggles. Sometimes I would get out of bed, go downstairs, and sob uncontrollably.

I missed my baby so much.

I knew that she was in heaven, and safe with Jesus. I believed that one day I would see her again. I had two beautiful children who filled my life with joy, and a husband whose love for me was never in question. Because of this, I felt so utterly ungrateful, and full of self-pity, in allowing my emotions to be get the better of me.

How dare I feel so sorry for myself when there were other couples who, for one reason or another, could never have a child of their own?

I read recently, on a card that I was given, that those who have lived in our hearts are never really gone; for love, which is timeless, never ceases to exist.

The love that I had for my baby was timeless and had never ceased to exist.

And yet I felt so full of guilt and regret.

There was a cloud of pain that enveloped me once again —an almost palpable thing that hung over me like a mist. At times those feelings became almost unbearable.

The overwhelming sadness became increasingly intense. But whenever that sadness floated to the surface, I kept trying to push it back down.

I remember as a child, when splashing around in the sea, trying with all of my strength to push my large, colourful beach ball down under the surf, only to have it bob up again the moment I took my hands off it.

The feeling was the same now. It was one of frustration, and a sense of getting nowhere fast. The next time the emotions floated up, there I was again, trying to achieve the impossible, all the while thinking to myself, 'Don't be so ridiculous. You have to let this go. Be grateful for what you have, and not what you have lost.'

On occasion, I would find that I was making myself think about the events that surrounded my daughter's birth and death, until the memory of it became too hard to bear.

Once again, I would dissolve into tears.

There were moments when I would be watching a film in which a miscarriage occurred, or a baby was stillborn, or a child died. I could rationalise my tears, both to my husband and to myself, by explaining, 'Oh, it's just that I'm too soft-hearted. I cry over anything remotely sad.' That, in part, was true.

But I knew that this was different.

These were tears of regret, of remorse, not simply of sadness and grief.

The same emptiness that I felt in the baby's nursery all those years ago was there again. In fact, it had never really left me.

There was the anger, too.

What was that about?

Who was I so angry at?

It was almost two years later, at Ben's sixth birthday party, that the turning point came.

After Chris completed his MA, he was accepted at Cambridge University to study for a PhD. We were so excited about the move to Cambridge. I had only ever visited there twice but had fallen for it hook, line, and sinker.

The history of that great city fascinated me. It was wonderful to feel just a tiny part of such a unique place, with its outstanding colleges and its beautiful river that ran alongside the famous 'Backs.' Here people would sit for hours, whiling away the time, relaxing and watching the punts go by.

We rented a small house just fifteen minutes or so from the city centre.

Katie settled happily into what was now her third school. How blessed we were to have such an easy-going child.

For Ben, it was his first experience of school. I will never forget taking him that first morning. He said nothing, but his fingers curled more and more tightly around my own as we reached the school's entrance. After his first day, and for several days afterwards, he was quieter, and I experienced the same tightening of his fingers around my hand each morning.

After the weekend, I went on the Monday morning to speak to Ben's teacher. I explained to her that although Ben said he was fine, I was a little concerned as he wasn't his usual chatty self. As we talked, it transpired that she was a Christian. She promised that she would pray for Ben. She then asked if she could pray with me, which she did. I found that to be a generous act, and a humbling experience.

The following day, as I walked Ben to school, we were only half way up the drive when he dropped my hand. His excited little voice chirped, 'Today we are collecting leaves, Mummy. When we have flattened them, I will be able to bring them home for you to put on the fridge.' Before I could even properly respond, he gave me a kiss, ran into his class, and that was that.

He had arrived.

I cried all the way home that day.

Why?

Because God had once again shown me His kindness through a most unexpected source: Ben's teacher—who was thrilled when I shared with her God's answer to her prayers.

I was also crying because my baby had now taken his first real steps of independence. I remembered once more that, although I was giving him roots, already, even at such a tender age, I was now starting to give him wings.

Our first two years in Cambridge were very happy ones. Both of the children liked their school, and we had found a super church where we soon all felt at home.

With both children at school, I now had time on my hands. I got involved in church life and a variety of activities. Yet, underneath, there was always the overwhelming sense of sadness that kept rising up to meet me.

Time on my hands was not good.

I needed to keep busy.

I was fortunate enough to secure a job as a nurse, working two days a week for Professor Steven Hawking. I loved that job. What an amazing and gracious man he was, with a fantastic sense of humour. In spite of being rather overawed at first—and the job certainly had its challenges— I learned a great deal about acceptance from Steven, as I had in a different way from Joni Eareckson Tada.

Those days were a real privilege for me. Not because I could say that I worked for the famous Steven Hawking, but supremely because of his generous nature.

Brilliant man that he is, he interacted warmly and graciously with those, like myself, of very average intellect, and in very ordinary jobs, compared to him. He never ever, as far as I witnessed, made anyone feel inferior.

I feel blessed to have known him. One thing my time working for this man taught me, with his brilliant mind housed in such a physically limited body, is that no disability can chain the human spirit, unless we allow it to.

Courage shows itself in a million different ways.

Working with Steven showed me just some of them.

* * * * *

It was a very, very hot day. As, with Katie's help, I put the final touches to Ben's birthday cake, we were both excited. I had made him a castle and Katie and I had been into Cambridge searching for knights and horses, to add the finishing touches to my masterpiece.

We were laughing away together because it was so hot outside that the castle turrets kept sliding off. In the end, they had to be secured with matchmaker chocolate sticks, which we kept eating.

We then decorated the room before Ben arrived with my friend and her two children. She had kindly taken them all off to the park, allowing me the space to get things ready. When Ben came into the lounge, he was thrilled as he spotted balloons and banners all around the room, and was delighted with his cake, with its sliding turrets.

The party was a great success, enjoyed by children and parents alike. By the time everyone was due to leave, the children were still going strong, and the parents were, yes, exhausted. Being good friends, however, they stayed to help us clear away, while Chris continued to entertain the children in the garden.

While we were clearing up, I went into the kitchen and happened to hear one friend remark, 'Yes, so much work. And then it all seems to be over in five minutes, doesn't it?'

Another friend observed, 'Yes, that's true. But it's worth all of the love and effort that you put in just to see their faces. And the truth is, you always have the memories to hold on to, don't you?'

As I listened, it was as if I was frozen to the spot.

'Memories to hold on to.'

Suddenly, in that one moment, I began to understand what the years of pain and grief that I had been constantly experiencing, since the death of our baby girl, had really been about.

I was shocked by the thoughts that came into my mind.

Feelings of guilt swept over me.

I knew that I could not think about this now.

This was Ben's day.

Nevertheless, I knew that one day—and very soon—I would have to face up to those feelings again, since it was becoming more and more difficult to ignore them.

The next few weeks were a busy time, as we had already begun to pack up our belongings once more. We were moving to another part of Cambridge for Chris to take up a post as Principal of Romsey House, a small independent theological college.

With the job came a terraced house that conveniently sat next to the college. Since a fair amount needed to be done in the house before we could move in, some dear friends who were going away on holiday kindly gave us the use of their home for a few weeks, while the more substantial work on the house was done.

Although there was a lot of hard work to be done, it was also fun. Moreover, in our busy-ness, grief was pushed away once more, until a more convenient time.

Finally, we moved into our newly-decorated home.

The children settled well. They moved to a small local school, which they really loved.

After so many moves, I at last felt settled.

And we were in fact to remain there for nine years. A record for us!

Life at Romsey House was a real blessing. So many people touched our lives in a variety of different ways during our time there. The children thrived, very much a part of the community, and they were spoiled rotten at times by staff and students alike. Nor were we ever short of baby-sitters!

All in all, it was a truly blessed and positive time for all of us.

Sure, there were hard times.

And tough lessons to learn.

Yet, looking back, I am so thankful that we were there.

18

MY HUGE BAG OF WORRIES

It was whilst we were at Romsey House that I first began working at the Children's Hospice in Milton, a village just outside of Cambridge.

In the course of my work there I became familiar with a wonderful book that we used when working with the siblings of terminally ill children. These children often had all kinds of worries and concerns over their sick brother or sister.

For various reasons, such worries were often not shared. Sometimes it was because it was too hard to express what they were feeling. They simply didn't know how to put into words such deep fears and feelings. At other times they didn't want to trouble their parents. Being aware of how anxious their parents were about their brother or sister, they were reluctant to give them something else to be concerned about. In some cases, they kept their feelings to themselves because they felt guilty that they themselves were healthy, whilst their sibling was sick.

These are some of the common reasons that children found it hard to discuss the worries they had. So, without any outlet, the burden of them would just grow, and grow— sometimes to the point of affecting their own health, and in some instances their behaviour.

The book we regularly used is called *The Huge Bag Of Worries*. It is the story of a little girl called Jenny.

Jenny was a happy little girl. She had a lovely family, and nice friends. And a dog called Loftus. Yet Jenny changed from being a happy girl, and became sad. The reason for this is that she worried, and worried, about everything: from her dog getting fleas, to poor marks at school. Jenny worried when her Mum and Dad had a little argument. She even worried about bombs and wars, when she saw things on the news.

One day, Jenny woke up and found a large bag sitting next to her bed. It was full of all her worries. The bag followed her everywhere. The more she worried, the bigger it got.

Jenny asked her brother for help, but he said he didn't know what she was talking about, as he didn't have any worries at all. She thought perhaps she could ask her Mum for help, but then imagined that she would probably say, 'You've got no worries that I can see. You're a lucky girl.' And so she decided not to tell her. Dad might know what to do. But then, she thought again. No. Dad had enough worries of his own. She couldn't ask him.

Every day, it got worse. The bag got bigger, and bigger. She couldn't sleep because it kept tossing and turning beside her each night. One morning, Jenny got up, got dressed and walked down the road. She'd had enough. The tears started rolling down her cheeks. She sat on a garden wall, and put her head in her hands. She thought she'd have to live with her now huge bag of worries forever.

Then Jenny heard a voice. Looking up, she saw the kindly face of the elderly lady who lived next door. 'Goodness!' she exclaimed. 'What on earth is that huge bag of worries doing there?' Through her tears, Jenny explained that she had been carrying the huge bag of worries around for weeks and the more she worried, the bigger it got.

'Now let's open it up, and see what's inside,' the elderly neighbour suggested. Jenny insisted that she couldn't. If she opened the bag, the worries might jump out. Who knew what might happen then?

'Nonsense,' maintained the lady. 'There's nothing a worry hates more than being seen. If you have any worries, however big or small, the secret is to let them out slowly, one by one. Then show them to someone else, who will help you, and they'll soon disappear.'

So Jenny opened the bag.

The elderly lady sorted the worries into groups. Jenny was astonished to see how much smaller they looked when they were out in the open. Not so scary at all.

Half of the worries disappeared immediately, because lots of worries evaporate when shown the light of day. Some went away because they belonged to other people, like her Mum and Dad, and were not for Jenny to worry about at all. Some were worries that everyone had from time to time— even Jenny's teacher, her friends, and her family.

The important thing that Jenny had learned was that sharing her worries made all the difference.

Soon the huge bag of worries was empty.

It then disappeared, as if it had never been there at all.

Whenever I think about that book, or read it again, I am reminded of how many times, and in how many ways, over seven years, I had dragged behind me my own huge bag of worries.

Month in, and month out.

Year in, and year out.

I knew I carried a burden of grief that had never really been acknowledged, or dealt with.

Was it fear?

Was it guilt?

What was it that stopped me sharing my worries?

Having the courage to bring them into the open?

God, in His mercy, was to show me, and give me the strength to face my fears. Strength to open the bag, and look inside.

It was a Friday, and I went into the kitchen to do some ironing. I find that watching television sometimes helps pass the time while doing this particular task. I switched on the television, and there was a documentary of some sort already on. It was just coming to an end. I knew that there was a film about to begin, so I let the end of the program run its course.

My mind was rather more on what I would make for tea than the documentary. But I suddenly became aware of the young couple on the screen. What caught my attention was that they were laying flowers on a tiny grave. I put the iron down, turned the sound up, and watched.

No words were uttered. As the couple walked away, hand in hand, the camera simply focused on the writing on the gravestone. It revealed that this child had been stillborn.

The now familiar feeling of dis-ease swept over me. I wanted to stop reading. But I couldn't. These are the words that were inscribed on the headstone:

Our precious baby Lucy.
You were never meant for this world.
When you opened your eyes for the first time,
  you were already in heaven.
We love you.
We value you.
We promise never to forget you.
You made us a Mummy and Daddy.
THANK YOU.

Those words, so very simple, spoke volumes to me that day.

Gentle music was playing, and the camera remained on the headstone.

I couldn't take my eyes off it.

The programme finished, and the adverts came on. I remember just staring at the screen, yet seeing nothing. I switched off the iron. Tears were already streaming down my face, and by the time I sank onto the sofa in the lounge, I was sobbing.

Once again, I was stepping out of the boat.

Yet all I was aware of this time was the menacing, cold, black water beneath.

I was not walking, but sinking.

God's timing was perfect, as the children were at a friend's house after school that day, where they were having tea. Sitting alone in the lounge, I felt completely numb as all the grief accumulated over the now many years seemed to flood my heart and soul.

My mind went back to the day of Ben's party, and my friend's innocent conversation. 'It's worth all of the love and effort that you put in just to see their faces. And the truth is, you always have the memories to hold on to, don't you?'

That was it.

I had absolutely no memories of my little girl.

Suddenly, I was awash with the most awful sense of guilt that I had abandoned my daughter.

For the first time, I was understanding what all of the pain and the worries of the past years had been about. I had pushed grief away so many times, because I was too afraid to face it. I knew that even if I opened my own particular bag of worries, it was too late—absolutely too late—to do anything about them.

The moment had passed all those years ago in that labour ward.

And there was no going back.

I began sobbing again until I could hardly breathe, asking the Lord, and my baby, to forgive me.

But I found no peace.

Chris arrived home and called out in his usual, cheery way. Then he came to find me. The moment he entered the room, he was beside me.

'What's happened?

What's wrong?'

'Nothing,' I uttered, not wanting to alarm him. 'Everyone is OK. It's just that . . .' And I was sobbing again in his arms, completely inconsolable. He just held me, and let me cry, which is what I needed at that moment.

Once I had calmed down a little, Chris suggested that he would make me a cup of tea, and then we could talk. I remember thinking, as he left the room, 'Not even a cup of tea can put this right.' Yet, somehow, the normality of it was comforting.

While waiting for Chris to return, I wondered how I could divulge what I had done—the awful mistake I had made—without him judging me as I was now judging myself.

And yet, as he sat beside me once again, and I looked into his concerned eyes, I knew there was nothing to fear. Whatever I might disclose, I felt completely secure in his love. My greatest concern was opening up old wounds for him, as well as myself. Nevertheless, I knew that it was now or never.

And never meant no forgiveness.

No peace.

We sat for a long time with very little said. Every time I started to speak, I would begin to sob again. Finally, the words came tumbling out of my mouth. Once I started, there was no stopping me. He had to hear it all.

I told Chris about the conversation at Ben's party, and the realisation that, since our baby had died I had always regretted the decisions I made about her all those years ago; that I felt completely trapped in my grief and guilt. Through racking sobs, I confessed to him that I believed that I had rejected my baby—utterly and completely rejected her—and that the guilt had become unbearable.

The awful thing was that I knew there was nothing to be done.

I could never now put right the wrong that I had done to her. What sort of mother does not even want to look at her baby? Where was any evidence that she had existed at all, except within our hearts?

If only I had held her.

Looked into her eyes, and declared to her that I loved her, as I had with Katie, and Ben, so many times.

Why did I let fear stop me, and rob her, and us, of that?

Nothing was ever too much trouble for my other two children. I loved them with all of my heart. There was evidence of that love everywhere you looked, and everyone who knew us could see it.

They had been so perfect when they were born. As they grew, I was so proud when I was out with them, or when people complimented me on them in any way. Their photographs, and their achievements, were displayed all over the house. No time spent with them ever felt wasted. There was no sacrifice made which was too great for their happiness.

This baby, on the other hand, had been born so horribly damaged. So disadvantaged, with no expectations for the wonderful future that I hoped for for Katie and Ben.

Where was the picture of her among those of our other children?

Didn't that speak of rejection?

What had I ever made for her?

Done for her?

Didn't that speak of rejection?

I had not even given her a funeral, or a service of thanksgiving for her little life. A life lived only in the womb, it's true, yet lived nonetheless.

I had never even said goodbye to her.

I was filled with a mixture of remorse and anger; anger only towards myself.

I have always been someone who believes in the importance of getting to know a person's name and trying to say it correctly. It is, for me, a part of how we can value people. I hate it if I haven't seen someone for a considerable amount of time, and cannot bring their name to mind.

Yet, in the case of my own daughter, I hadn't even given her the same consideration. We had always simply called her 'our baby,' or 'our little girl.' Why had I not given her the dignity of having a name, at the very least?

After Ben was born, Katie would occasionally ask about

her little sister, but I never actively pursued any conversation about her; especially after her first birthday, and first Christmas, had passed. We had never really spoken to Ben about her very much at all, other than to say he had had a baby sister who had died and was in heaven with Jesus.

For Katie, especially, I felt I had not given her the chance to say goodbye to her sister. Katie had been there throughout it all. It was not that I felt she had been scarred emotionally, or any such thing, because of that decision. It was imply that she, together with us, should have been given the opportunity.

Yes, it was as if our daughter had never existed.

Yet I knew that she had.

And that she did, even now.

I had cherished her in the womb. I had wanted this child so much. I loved her still. That is why I was in so much pain, now. I longed to hold her, kiss her, tell her I was proud of her and that I was sorry for letting her down.

I cannot begin to describe the pain and grief in mere words.

I simply knew that, seven years before, I had got it so very wrong. The voices in my head shouted it out loud and clear. I felt as though I was in a crowd, being crushed, almost suffocated, by my own guilt and regret. I realised afresh that I had been carrying a huge burden of guilt, without even fully being aware of it.

Yet, what was to be done?

Nothing.

I could not say goodbye, or put things right.

It was all too late.

And the regret was overwhelming.

As we sat, uninterrupted, we wept together. Hearing the words coming out of my own mouth, almost as a confession, was somehow therapeutic. Chris then admitted that he himself had had regrets over the decisions made that day, but had never felt it fair to give them a voice. I smiled, knowing that for me it had been the same.

As I looked up at him, he quietly but firmly insisted, 'But they were *our* decisions, not just yours. And we made them under the most painful and difficult of circumstances.'

Chris went on to reveal that after I had had the baby he had gone to my sister's and tearfully shared with her his fears, not just for our baby, but also, at the height of my traumatic labour, for me. He recounted to me how he had confided to her that at one point he thought that he was going to lose us both.

He confessed to me that even in his deepest sorrow at the thought of our baby dying, his greatest concern, as he had watched me haemorrhaging, had been for me, and not the baby. In the early days after her death, there had then been times that he had felt guilty for that—as if the baby didn't matter.

But, of course, she did.

As he held me, we began together to reflect back on those early worries and concerns about my pregnancy. We recalled the devastating news that the scan had revealed. We reminded ourselves how, despite the kindness the staff at the hospital had shown us, we had been offered so little by way of emotional support.

We had received no advice on how to cope in such tragic circumstances. There had been no pre-bereavement counselling about the value of holding our dead child, or the possibility of creating even a few precious memories with her. There had been no one to advise on the actual benefits of holding our own special service for our baby.

It was painful, and yet at the same time helpful, to look back together. It was something, incredibly, that we had never done before.

I have come to understand since that we needed someone to guide us. Someone to give us permission, almost, to create those memories, even though our child had been stillborn. Someone to point out that we still needed a proper ending, and a time to say goodbye.

We needed to be helped through the grieving process.

At the time, it had felt to us more like it being about getting things over and done with, with a minimum of emotional pressure on all concerned. This was not due to a lack of care from the hospital staff. As I noted earlier, it was more the consequence of a relative lack of awareness and training in matters of loss and grief, compared to what is available now.

My friend Carol knew, when she had encouraged us to hold our baby, what the value to us might have been. However, at the time, fear, shock, and exhaustion had taken over. Perhaps, had Carol been stood next to me that day in the labour ward, it might have been different.

Who knows?

I only knew that we couldn't go back and retrace the steps, however much our hearts desired it.

Nevertheless, I suddenly didn't feel so alone. Understanding that Chris had had doubts of his own, and his utterly loyal insistence in reminding me, time and time again, that we had made all of our decisions together, gave me some comfort.

The children arrived home, tired and happy. They both looked concerned when they saw my red, bloated face from several hours of crying. Chris explained that I had been very upset about something but that it was going to be alright. We would talk with them about it, but another day.

They both gave me a big hug, and went upstairs to get ready for bed, rather more subdued than usual. Even at times such as those you can find yourself smiling. And we did, as we heard Katie shushing Ben, chiding in hushed, but very grown-up terms, 'Mum and Dad need some adult time. So don't make a fuss.'

With the children safely tucked into bed, we prayed together. As Chris held my hand, sensing that I was emotionally exhausted, he sensibly advised that there be no more talking that night. It was a comfort to feel him gently taking control. I tried to pray, but ended up sobbing instead.

My tear jar was filled to the brim.

But God didn't need my words.

He knew my heart.

And at that point, that was all that really mattered.

I found it hard to sleep that night. As I lay thinking about our conversation, I still felt both angry with myself, and guilty. I quietly slipped out of bed and went downstairs. Whatever Chris had asserted about decisions we had made together, Satan kept throwing at me thoughts that deeply troubled. 'Yes, you know deep down that if you had made a different decision that day, Chris would have supported you in that as well. Then you wouldn't have rejected your own baby, would you?'

And so the anger at myself grew.

During my time at the Hospice, I sometimes worked with the siblings of the sick children, as I touched on earlier. Some of that work was simple anger management.

One approach we used was to sit with the child, or a small group of children, and let them write on a piece of paper, or draw, anything that they felt angry about. When they had finished, we would talk through with them any issues this raised, if they wished to.

We would then take a big bag of clay and go to a quiet part of the Hospice grounds where there was an old brick wall on which the children stuck their sheet of paper with blue-tac. Taking large handfuls of clay, they would shout out their feelings of anger. As they shouted, they threw the clay as hard as they could, eventually knocking their sheet of paper off the wall.

Some of the things they shouted were unexpected, and powerful. Until then, I was unaware that a child—some only five or six years old—could feel such pent up rage. Witnessing this was a genuine privilege, as well as being utterly heart-rending. These were the tangible expressions of such deep pain.

Afterwards, we would collect all of the clay and the papers from the ground. The children shredded the paper, if they wanted to; though some of the older children chose to keep theirs so that they could later talk to their parents about it.

After a drink and some nice treats, we would divide up the clay and each of them would create something out of it that was positive for them. Something that would remind them of their brother, or sister. This was a time for fun and laughter at the masterpieces that were created. Next, the object they had made would be painted. Later, it was fired and glazed for them. It was then proudly taken home.

Many a parent later confided that their child had subsequently shared with them their experience. So doing had actually helped them, the parent, with their own feelings of anger, frustration, and guilt.

I knew that God did not want me to hold onto my feelings of anger and guilt.

They were destructive and unhelpful.

As I sat downstairs in the early hours, hugging a cup of tea, I knew that He could free me from this overwhelming feeling of suffocation, and from the voices accusing me in my head. I prayed for a word to encourage me.

I picked up my Bible and started flicking through the pages, opening it up in Mark's Gospel. My eyes were drawn to the latter part of chapter five, which I had underlined at some point. They came to rest on verses 23 and 24. 'My little daughter is dying. Please come and put your hands on her so that she will be healed and live.' So Jesus went with Jairus, the one making this request of him.

My honest first reaction was a feeling of frustration that this wasn't particularly helpful. As wonderful as this outcome was for Jairus and his daughter, it felt as though this was actually rubbing salt into my wound right then.

As I read on, however, I came to the story of the woman

who had suffered from haemorrhaging for twelve years. I was deeply touched afresh by this woman's story. Her courage, and determination to battle through the suffocating heat and crowds to get to Jesus, were quite amazing. How weak she must have felt after suffering from such a debilitating illness for so long.

And yet she kept going.

She knew her only hope was to get to Him. Even to touch the hem of His garment would be enough. As she did, He felt the power go from Him. That prompted the question that amazed His disciples: 'Who touched me?'

'You see the people crowding against you, and yet you can ask, "Who touched me?"' they countered.

The next verse was so precious to me as I read on. 'But Jesus kept looking around to see who had done it.'

Jesus knew that this had been a touch of faith from an unseen person in the crowd.

He could have just walked on.

But He didn't.

He wanted to face the person; to value and encourage them by addressing them directly. It was a personal response that came out of a relationship defined by faith.

I was surprised at the reading the Lord had shown me. Perhaps I had expected something about anger, or feeling guilty. Yet the Lord knew that it was renewed faith in His ability to love me and bring me through my pain that was needed here.

I felt so humbled by this woman.

As I wept and prayed, I was reminded that night that faith is not just about big gestures, and the moving of mountains. It is also about simply reaching out, in all of our fear, and touching the hem of His garment.

And when I reached out to him that night, the voices in my head disappeared.

It was just He and I.

For the first time in a long time I could breathe again.

I was no longer suffocated by guilt, and the anger had abated.

Healing had begun.

Tomorrow, I knew, would be different.

And it was.

* * * * *

I love the fable of the Cold North Wind and the Gentle Sun:

> *The north wind and the sun were arguing one day as to who possessed the greatest power. 'Observe,' said the north wind. 'Observe that man down there. See how easily I shall blow his coat from off his shoulders.' So the north wind blew icier and icier, but the man simply wrapped his coat even tighter around his shoulders. And then the sun gently said, 'Now you've had your opportunity, please, allow me to try.' And so the sun shone, gentle and warm, and the man took off his coat.*

I have been blessed so many times by the gentle touch of God's power in my life.

Never accusing, always loving.

It's certainly true that there have been times when He has given me a good talking to. Just as with any loving parent, there will be a need at times for the chastising of their child. And yet, even at such times as those, I have, like the man who shed his coat, felt there was no longer a need to wrap it tighter and tighter around my shoulders for protection and comfort.

For His gentleness has provided me with all that I have needed, or, I believe, will ever need.

The following morning, it was raining hard. Yet it just didn't seem to matter. As I was making coffee, and waiting for Chris to come downstairs, I felt a renewed sense of hope and peace for the future.

The moment he arrived in the kitchen, I excitedly began to fill him in on my time with the Lord. He was both thrilled and relieved that I was feeling so much more positive.

Once the children were up and sorted, they went off to play in their rooms. Katie looked at my still swollen eyes and enquired, 'Are you all right, Mummy?' I assured her that I was, but that there was something her Dad and I needed to discuss. Later we would have a family time together and explain why I had been so upset the previous day. This seemed to allay her concerns.

I knew now that it was not too late to change things, to put things right. If God could heal a woman of a terrible illness through a simple touch of faith, He could find a way to help us move forward through our grief.

We had made mistakes, we felt, but perhaps He could use even those to glorify His name. Maybe others had found themselves in similar circumstances, and we could use our experiences to help them. Suddenly, I knew that all this had been for a reason. What that reason was, I wasn't yet sure.

But, as we took one step at a time, He would show us.

Of that I was now certain.

For a good deal of that day, we talked, we cried, but we also laughed. And I was to learn that it is never too late to grieve, to put right wrongs, to endure.

Never too late to hope again.

That night, my reading was from Psalm 18. It was verses 16-19 that really spoke to me.

He reached down from on high and took hold of me;
* he drew me out of deep waters.*
He rescued me from my powerful enemy,
* from my foes, who were too strong for me.*
They confronted me in the day of my disaster,
* but the LORD was my support.*
He brought me out into a spacious place;
* he rescued me because he delighted in me.*

What a promise He gave me that night.

I was reminded of it many years later when someone passed on to me a short extract from an article they had been given, by Max Lucado.

'Because He delights in me' (Ps.18:19)

And you thought He saved you because of your decency. You thought He saved you because of your good works or good attitude, or good looks. Sorry. If that were the case, your salvation would be lost when your voice went south or your works got weak. There are many reasons God saves you: to bring glory to Himself, to appease His justice, to demonstrate His sovereignty. But one of the sweetest reasons God saved you is because He is fond of you. He likes having you around. He thinks you are the best thing to come down the pike in quite a while, 'As a man rejoices over his new wife, so your God rejoices over you.' (Isaiah.62:5) If God had a refrigerator, your picture would be on it. If He had a wallet, your photo would be in it. He sends you flowers every spring and a Sunrise every morning. Whenever you want to talk, He'll listen. He can live anywhere in the universe, and He chose your heart. And the Christmas gift He sent you from Bethlehem? Face it friend. He's crazy about you.

I smiled as I read this, for He had proved so many times, and in so many different ways, just that.

So why should I doubt it?

19

GRACE

I once saw a beautiful documentary about baby eagles. They were born in the most amazing nests, high up in the mountains. When they were still very young, their mother would nudge them out of the nest, and they would begin to fall to the ground, their wings not yet strong enough to enable them to fly.

I watched, horrified, as they seemed to hurtle to the ground. Then, all of a sudden, their mother was there, swooping down from the nest towards them. Flying underneath her babies, she would scoop them up onto her huge outspread wings, and carry them back up to the nest, and to safety. This would happen time after time, until the day came when she no longer had to save them, because, as they were falling, their wings began to flap, and they were strong enough, and brave enough, to fly by themselves, and be free.

What a lesson this was for me.

For so long I had not felt free, but rather in free-fall, my guilt not allowing me the dignity of grief. After the past few days, I felt as though I had been pushed out of the nest so many times. Yet I was thankful that, instead of hitting the ground, I had found a safe place to land.

Frightening as it had been to feel out of control, I was aware of His everlasting arms underneath me. I knew that I now needed to trust Him enough to be able to take flight and play my own part in finding freedom from remorse and guilt.

And so, on that Saturday morning, with the rain beating against the windows, Chris and I sat together and talked. We both had a positive feeling that we were about to find a way forward. And I knew, even at this early stage, that the healing process had begun.

But what to do first?

Where were we to begin?

The most important thing emerging for both of us was that we wanted to give our little girl a name. An identity. We thought about several, but there was really only one name that had been on my heart.

Grace.

Chris loved it, and we very easily came to a decision together about that being right.

So we named our beautiful baby girl 'Grace.'

Grace had been given to us for a very special reason. Just as God's grace in our lives is a gift, so we believed that our daughter's life was also a gift from Him. She had been given to us for a purpose, though what that purpose was, we were not yet sure.

Once her name was chosen, I was thrilled, and found myself saying it over and over in my head.

Our daughter, Grace. God's gift to us.

It was perfect.

Next, we felt that we wanted to give thanks in some way for Grace's life. We also wanted to include the children in this. This wasn't just about us, but them, too. It was important to us that we acknowledge Grace's birth, and her death, as a family, so that together we could experience a proper ending, a proper goodbye.

I saw so many precious things while working at the Children's Hospice. With the permission of the parents concerned, I recall some pertinent ones below. These real-life stories show us that goodbyes and endings are so important as part of the grief process, and that these times can be such a blessing when facing a future without a loved one.

There were times when I was privileged to help parents

organise their child's funeral. This was invariably a most precious and uplifting experience. You may be thinking, 'Uplifting? A child's funeral? Impossible!' And yet it was wonderfully true.

I remember one little girl who came from a family of travellers. Her mum belonged to a Pentecostal Church, and her Pastor took the girl's funeral service in the chapel in the cemetery grounds.

Whilst we stood waiting for the family to arrive, gradually the area filled with dozens of travellers who had come from around the country to attend the service. They couldn't all fit into the little chapel since there must have been a hundred of them there, in the end. So they stood silently outside, with their own children beside them, and babies in their arms.

Following a wonderful service of thanksgiving, the little girl's coffin was carried towards the grave as everyone sang *He's got the whole world in his hands* at the top of their voices. The travellers didn't come to the graveside, but stood in the cemetery, completely silent, with their heads bowed.

After the committal, dozens of colourful balloons with loving messages on them were released into the air. As we watched them rise, I turned to look back at the chapel, which was only a few hundred yards away.

To my utter amazement, every single traveller had gone. It was almost as if they had disappeared. There had been no sound. No evidence of any movement. They had simply vanished, as though they had never been there. They had come to say goodbye in their own way. Quietly, and with dignity, they had then departed.

I found it a deeply moving experience.

I was beginning to learn that people have different ways of grieving, and saying goodbye. There is in fact no right or wrong way. Each experience is quite unique. And precious.

My next account powerfully demonstrates this point. It also underlines the value and significance of memories, something I wrote about earlier. As we shall see, these can be important even at the end of a life.

A family at the Hospice knew that their little girl did not have long to live. All their hopes were pinned on the fact that she might make it to Christmas, since this was her very favourite time of year. However, towards the end of October her health suddenly deteriorated and she was admitted to the local hospital.

The family wanted to move her to the Hospice, but she was simply too poorly to make the journey to Cambridge. They so wanted her to make it to Christmas, yet, as they observed her rapidly failing health, they began to realise that this was now highly unlikely.

Faced with this prospect, my colleague and I put to the staff on the hospital ward the possibility of celebrating Christmas early. The girl was in a side room, so it wouldn't disturb anyone else, and it would mean so much to the family. Was there any way we could make this happen?

The staff were unsure at first, but after further discussion agreed. We talked the possibility through with the parents. They, and their young son, were thrilled. Once the decision had been made, it was all systems go; all hands on deck. Everyone seemed to catch the vision.

The parents watched with fascination as their daughter's room was transformed into a Christmas grotto. Everyone got on board, even the Senior Paediatrician. We went out and bought some little gifts and other items, for once delighted that these days, in some of the shops at least, Christmas starts in September.

The nurses found a Christmas tree stored away, and some decorations. Perched on top of the tree was a wobbly angel with a broken halo which made everyone hoot with laughter, even at such a difficult and sad time. It was all wonderfully glitzy and tasteless, with tinsel strewn everywhere. There were even fairy lights at the window.

One of the doctors bought a little Christmas cake from a local shop, while the hospital kitchen staff provided drinks and nibbles for everyone. Mum and Dad had brought in some Disney Christmas music, the girl's favourite. All in all, within a very short time the transformation was complete. There were even Christmas cards made by some of the staff.

It was October 23rd, and the parents decided this was going to be their Christmas Eve.

They knew that time was running short.

That night they all stayed at the hospital in readiness for the big day. The following day dawned and throughout October 24th, their Christmas day, visitors, friends and hospital staff all stopped by for a visit. Their little girl drifted in and out of sleep, but was aware enough to take in when she had a gift to open, or some carols were sung.

In the evening, the whole family snuggled up on the bed together. The visitors left, and it was just their time.

Time to say goodbye.

A few minutes before midnight, their precious daughter left them. She slipped quietly and peacefully from this life, into the next.

A few days later, when I met with the girl's parents, they gratefully acknowledged the gift they had been given that day. Although their hearts were broken, they had been given one last Christmas: the chance to say goodbye as they had wished.

I visited the family the following Christmas. They had put up decorations. In pride of place, on top of the tree, was the wobbly angel. As I looked at it, I smiled. The girl's mum related to me how the nurses had insisted she take it home. When they popped it on the top of the tree, they were so very thankful that the memory of that day would never be lost.

A precious day. A happy day, despite everything.

It was, she concluded, a day to remind them every year to be thankful that their daughter had been, for just a short while, theirs.

It is important not only for us as adults to say goodbye,

but also for children. It was such a privilege for me to meet some of the siblings of sick children at the Hospice. They helped me to understand that you can never be too young to say goodbye to a loved one.

I was astonished, at times, by the way that some of the children—even as young as four—coped with death. And how, while being supported and protected, they could be offered the opportunity to say goodbye, so being helped in some measure to come to terms with what had happened within their family.

A tiny baby with a very poor prognosis was transferred to us from a London hospital. He had a very serious illness for which, sadly, there was no successful treatment. I was on duty the afternoon the family arrived in the ambulance. They looked both shocked and terrified.

After settling them in, they started to relax a little. Within a few days they were feeling more comfortable and able to talk about their feelings. They knew that their little boy might only live for a few weeks, if that, and they asked if they could have him christened at the Hospice.

The christening was to be on the Sunday, three days later. Knowing that they had two other children, who were staying with their grandparents, I asked them if they would be coming. The mum replied that she whilst would like them to come, she believed it was better for them if they didn't get to know their little brother as he would die so soon. She felt it wasn't fair on them.

Although I fully understood this mum's predicament, I gently suggested to her how it could be helpful for them to meet, and get to know, their brother, even if only for a short while. They would then have some memories of him in the future. I explained that honesty and openness are important to children, even at such times as these.

Making them a part of his life now could help them later.

Despite raising these considerations with her, I was careful to explain to this struggling mum that it was absolutely her and her husband's decision. I pointed out that at such times there are really no right or wrong ways, but that people have to go with the decision that they deem right for them, and that they find a measure of peace in.

The following day she sought me out. She had shared our conversation with her husband and they both now felt that they wanted their other children, a little girl of four and a boy of seven, to come and meet their brother.

The hour before the children arrived, the parents were quite nervous. Nevertheless, once their little ones came bouncing in, they knew that, for them, this was right. Both children held their tiny little brother. They cried when their mum and dad explained that he would go to heaven in a short while, because he was very poorly. From that moment on, however, the whole family stayed together at the Hospice.

The children helped with their brother's care, and the christening was a day of celebration. As their brother's condition deteriorated, they went with their mum to choose a special, 'cool' outfit for him to wear for his funeral.

Some weeks later, the baby died.

His brother and his little sister were there with their mum and dad when he slipped way from them. Having had it explained to them how he might look, and feel, after death, there was no fear for them. He was still simply their baby brother.

One of the most moving moments of my time at the Hospice was when the family was waiting for the car to come that would collect the baby's little body and take it to the chapel of rest.

The children were in the Hospice lounge, where the play-leader was reading them a story, when mum and dad called them to come and say goodbye to their brother. They entered the bedroom where he lay in his Moses basket. On the bed was a beautiful knitted baby blanket that the parents had been using to cuddle him in while at the Hospice. It was special to them both, as it had also belonged to their other children when they were babies.

As the little girl said goodbye, she put her own little teddy in the basket. The seven year old boy went up to the basket, leaned over it, and kissed his brother on the forehead. Then, picking up the soft, fluffy blanket, he tucked it around his little body. Finally, as the tears slid down his cheeks, he drew the blanket right over his face, so tenderly, and told him that he loved him.

We all cried, then, for the loss of such a beautiful child.

But there was more than that.

For in that one precious moment we had witnessed a most beautiful picture of innocence and love. And so, in the years to come, both children were able to remember their brother. Much later, they each expressed to their parents, in their own way, that they were glad that they had known him, and had had the opportunity, when the time came, to say goodbye.

To say a proper goodbye is important—for adults, and for children.

* * * * *

This was the time to talk to our children about their sister Grace, and to decide together how our goodbye might be said. So we sat down with Katie and Ben, recounting briefly what had happened when Grace had died and how Chris and I both had regrets over the decisions we had made that day.

They were so sweet. They sat there, quietly listening, as we explained everything. We informed them of the name we had given her. They both loved it. Ben suggested that one day he might write a letter to her. That would be lovely, we responded, if that was what he wanted to do.

We went on to explain to them that since Grace hadn't had a funeral service, we wanted now to do something for her.

Something that would allow us all to say goodbye.

They really liked that idea and we chatted for a while, thinking around possibilities of what we might do. I was quite touched by their enthusiasm. Katie thought it would be nice to do something that Grace would have liked. Ben thought she would have liked to go for an ice cream, which gave us all a laugh. After a time, a plan had been formulated that seemed good to all of us.

The following Saturday, a beautiful, sunny winter's day, we went together to Grantchester, a delightful village on the outskirts of Cambridge. There is a path there that runs alongside the river; somewhere we often walked on Sunday afternoons, particularly in the summer time. It is a lovely spot that we appreciated and valued as a family.

On the way, we stopped off at a florist's where we bought three of the most beautiful crimson roses.

Arriving at Grantchester, we parked the car and walked down by the river. We soon came to an area where there were ducks and swans in abundance, all swimming around, enjoying the winter sun. We had come equipped with enough bread to feed an army. Ben thought Grace would have liked that. As we threw the bread onto the water, yet more ducks arrived, seemingly out of nowhere. Some bravely mounted the bank, where they were even prepared to feed from our hands.

There were lots of smiles.

It was a happy moment shared together.

Chris then offered a few simple but precious thoughts about Grace, and her coming into our lives. He prayed a prayer of thanksgiving for her life and the fact that she was now safe in the arms of Jesus.

I then gave Katie and Ben a rose each, whilst Chris and I held onto ours together.

Twice around the time of losing Grace I had been blessed, in moments of great sadness, by three roses that became for me a part of God's compassionate provision. First, in the dingy cafeteria after first hearing Grace's diagnosis. And then in the solitude of my hospital room. That is why we considered them the appropriate flower now to remember Grace by.

As we held our roses, we told Grace that we loved her.

In saying our goodbyes, we were also saying, 'We will never forget you.'

As my fingers brushed the delicate, velvety petals, it felt so different from those other times. I knew that I had found peace at last, and could finally forgive myself, and be free from guilt.

We threw roses on the river for Grace that day.

We walked along the riverbank, following their path. Two roses that had drifted further out floated swift and free. One, however, became tangled in some branches and we had to clamber down the bank to free it with a stick.

I was reminded that life is like that. Sometimes, it is just plain sailing, whilst at other times we end up getting stuck, and need a little help to become free again. I silently thanked God that He had reached down and untangled me.

And, on that particular day, he had set me free.

Afterwards, we walked back to a place called the Orchard; a wonderful tearoom by the river, that sits in an enormous orchard. Hence, the name! We had tea and cakes, and Ben had his ice cream.

We talked.

We laughed.

We celebrated Grace's all-too-brief life.

As we later made our way home, I was happy to be with my family: my husband, and my three children—two in the car with us, and one in heaven.

From time to time we find ourselves back in Cambridge. Occasionally, we go to the Orchard and it is lovely to stroll along the riverside to where, for us, is Grace's spot. We have sometimes even fed the ducks, recalling that this is where memories of our daughter were created, and where we promised her, on that day, that she would never be forgotten.

Since I had nothing tangible of Grace's to keep, Chris came up with a lovely idea. He suggested that we buy a simple gold band, on the inside of which I could have Grace's name engraved. I loved the idea as it meant that I would be able to wear it all the time, and she would somehow always feel a part of me.

While we were out together a few weeks later, I spotted a ring in a jeweller's shop window. It was rose gold. I loved its rich warm colour and the fact that it was quite distinctive from my wedding ring, which I wanted to wear it next to.

Reflecting on what to have engraved on the ring, I wanted more than just Grace's name. We finally settled on the right words.

'Grace. God's gift to us.'

So, the following day, I went into town to have the ring engraved. I was served by the manager of the shop. He enquired how he could help. As I started to explain what I wanted, to my absolute horror, I began to cry. He was so kind as I managed to get myself together and to briefly sketch the circumstances.

He quite understood my being upset, and was very sympathetic. He thought the idea was a lovely one. He assured me that they would engrave the ring to the highest standards. I confess that I left the shop feeling a little foolish, despite his kind words. Nevertheless, I couldn't wait for the ring to be ready.

When I went to collect the ring a short while later, the manager happened to be in the shop once again. He fetched the ring for me, smiling all over his face as I looked at it. It was perfect. So beautifully engraved. As I slipped it on my finger, next to my wedding band, I knew that was where it would stay.

And so it has, ever since.

As I was paying, the manager looked up at me. 'I hope you don't mind, Mrs. Jack, but my niece went through a similar experience to you last year. I told her about your ring. She thought the idea was so lovely that she is going to do the same thing on her little boy's first anniversary.'

'Mind?' I replied. 'I am delighted.'

As I walked out of the shop, my heart was singing.

I thought to myself, 'Yes, Grace. You are already making a difference.'

As Grace's mum, I felt that I had never been able to give her anything, or do anything for her, as I had for my other children. This was important to me and I was determined not to let the circumstances of her birth and death stop me. So I determined to make her a gift. I didn't have a photo of her, and could only imagine in my head what she might have looked like.

Well, I thought, if I can't have a photo, I can create a picture.

And that is what I did.

I decided to embroider a fine cross-stitch picture. It is of a baby girl in a crib. I did not want any dates on it, as it is not a memorial plaque. To me, it is simply a memory of our precious little girl that I was able to create. On it, are embroidered the words:

OUR DAUGHTER GRACE. GOD'S GIFT TO US.

The embroidery took me eighteen months to complete, but every stitch was made with love. Doing it was actually very therapeutic. Once finished, I had it framed, and it hangs on the wall in our lounge.

Everything that I have written in this chapter is a proof that it is never too late to grieve, or to find peace with ourselves. All those years ago, for a variety of reasons we felt we had made mistakes that could never be rectified.

How very wrong we were.

You may recall that I mentioned above Ben suggesting to us that one day he would write a letter to his sister.

Some years later, he did.

Grace. A Few Questions.

Hello there big sister,
How are you today?
I guess I've never really talked with you
Like a brother and sister would.

I'm sorry to say it's been a while.
Since I held you in my thoughts, that is.
I don't expect you'll take offence,
For I feel I know you better than that.

Do you, as I, ever wonder
How different things could be?
Strange to think of parenting hours,
Lost for you, hopefully not wasted on me.

Something I've always wondered:
Who would you have been more like?
Your sister Katie, or me?
And would we have been friends, or only siblings?
I think we would have been both.

Would we have talked about girlfriends and boyfriends?
Would you have laughed when I told you a joke?
Would you have cried when things got you down?
Would you have helped me gang up on Mum and Dad?
And would you have grown up into the young woman I see now?

Such questions I'm sure you smile upon.
But think hard for me, because I know for sure

Such questions we will chat about,
When I come home and meet our mutual friends.

Well, I'll go now,
But I'll be back again soon for an update.
Before I go, Grace, just one last question,
If I may.

Dear sister, I ask you,
Rhetorically, if you please:
Do you know that Mum and Dad love you?
As do I, and Katie.

Always.

20

ROSES ON THE RIVER

Some years later, while working at the Children's Hospice, I was given the opportunity to attend a conference on the effects that guilt can have on the way we grieve. It was held at Lee Abbey, a Christian Conference Centre in Devon. The house itself was lovely, but it was the setting that made it special. Surrounded by hills and the sea, with waves lapping into small, secluded coves along the shoreline, it was breathtaking.

The seminars were stimulating as we were taken on a journey of how guilt can often have a lasting negative effect on the grief process. On the penultimate evening, opportunity was given for people to share their own stories. These touched our emotions at the deepest level.

As the evening went on, I felt that the Lord wanted me to related my own experience of guilt over Grace. However, up to that point I had only articulated this deeply personal experience to a very few people—mainly family and a small number of close friends.

To even contemplate standing up in front of two hundred people that I barely knew was daunting. My mouth was dry, and my heart was pounding as I stood to my feet. All I could hear in my head were my friend's words, to which I made reference in an earlier chapter. 'What does God want from you the most? He wants your weakness. For His strength is made perfect in weakness.'

As I started to speak, I was aware of His strength holding me up on nervous, shaky legs. I told my story simply and from the heart. When I sat down, the tears ran unchecked down my cheeks. Not because I was sad. But because I had given Grace the opportunity to reach out to others through her story.

And it felt so precious to me.

The evening ended, and refreshments were served. While everyone chatted away to one another, a doctor, who was one of the speakers at the conference, came over to me. He thanked me for the things I had shared about Grace. He then added, 'Can I encourage you, one day, to write it all down in a book?' I thanked him, protesting, quite genuinely, that I could never write a book.

Although I had kept notes of many of my experiences, as well as my spiritual and emotional journey through that time, that was, for me, as far as it would go. He encouraged me to think about it as he believed the Lord wanted those thoughts and experiences to be communicated more widely.

I was so touched by his words and briefly thought, 'Maybe one day. Who knows?'

We left after lunch the following day. As I got into my car to drive away, it struck me that, in all, twelve women had come to speak with me about the things I had shared the evening before.

I was astonished that so many others had carried guilt, some for many years, over issues very similar to my own. Some had experienced miscarriages. Others, stillbirths. Two had borne children and had them adopted. There were those who disclosed that their other children, now grown up, had never even known that they had had a brother or sister.

I was overwhelmed with sadness as I listened to their different accounts.

Some stated that they were going home to talk with their husbands and children, to find a way of saying goodbye to their own little ones. Others had found comfort in the fact that, like Chris and I, they hadn't been aware that there was any other way. Simply being able to accept that fact had eased their pain and guilt.

Twelve women, out of two hundred, had come to talk

with me—all a similar age to myself, or older.

How many more were there out there?

Still grieving.

Still carrying a burden of guilt.

During the years that followed, I had the immense privilege of being involved in providing counselling and pastoral support in many different contexts. I was to hear many heart-breaking stories of women who had been touched in one way or another so deeply by guilt and grief.

Some, for different reasons, had undergone abortions and were now living with the guilt of those decisions, made long ago. The stories of these women who had terminated their pregnancy were amongst the hardest to listen to. Some had made their decision before they were Christians; some afterwards.

What they all had in common was the belief, at the time, that this was the only solution to their particular situation and problems. Yet many subsequently came to believe that they had made a mistake. And they were desperate, now, to say sorry and to find forgiveness from their dead children, and from God Himself.

They longed to find an end to their individual pain.

Many confessed that even though they had brought their burden of guilt to God, they were still bound, years later, by guilt. They were bound, when the Lord Himself wanted them to be free.

I knew so well how that felt.

I was taken back in my mind, on many an occasion, to the documentary on the baby eagles to which I referred earlier. Reflecting on it, I was led to write a simple poem— almost as a prayer—for all the women who had shared their stories with me.

FORGIVEN

I was feeling so weary, and so full of shame,
For all of the wrong I had done;

Tired and tormented, and longing to blame
Someone else for the wretch I'd become.
Knowing I'd wasted such valuable time,
And squandered the life I'd been given,
I heard a small voice, saying, 'Child don't despair!'
And He whispered the words, 'You're forgiven.'

Forgiven? Lord, me? With my terrible past?
Surely God couldn't overlook that?
One so powerless and weak couldn't sit at His feet;
Could your love, Lord, for me really last?
I want to be used, but I haven't the strength;
Can your power really touch such as I?
As I stand on the edge of this faltering ledge,
Could it be, Lord, with you I can fly?

Fear not, you're forgiven. Let His peace fill your heart;
Your past is now hidden in Him.
And as far as the east from the west is removed,
He'll no longer remember your sin.
You're forgiven, it's true; with such knowledge as this,
Just to know that for you He did die,
He has taken your pain, do not live it again,
Like the eagle, you're free—you can fly!

Grace's story became, in a remarkable way, a source of blessing and encouragement to others as I became more ready to tell it, when appropriate. To some, in particular, it offered a measure of comfort and a ray of hope.

On one occasion, I was providing support to a woman with three children who was an artist. Many years before, at just sixteen years of age, she had terminated twins. Now in her forties, she was still struggling with her guilt, feeling that she did not even have the right to grieve for them.

After several sessions with her, I felt that God was prompting me to share with her about Grace. I did. When we finished, she expressed a strong sense of renewed hope, given her by identifying with aspects of the story I had recounted, and she left feeling more peaceful.

Several months later, I had a phone call from the woman, asking if she could come to see me. When she arrived, she was carrying a large package. She wanted to show me something. As she lifted the large item out and handed it to me, I came face to face with a most beautiful picture that she had painted herself.

The painting was of the outstretched hands of a very young girl. The tender hands were reaching out towards a simple wooden cross. Nestled in the hands were two tiny babies. You couldn't make out the whole shape of the babies. Just their heads, their soft downy hair, and the tops of their tiny shoulders. The painting gave the impression of two tiny little souls being offered back to God, through the cross.

It was so incredibly beautiful.

I was overwhelmed.

The woman then began to relate how she had gone home the day I had shared with her about Grace, and had divulged her past to her husband and children. She felt she could no longer keep this secret. Understandably, her husband's first reaction was shock. Nevertheless, he and her children had been wonderfully supportive of her. In fact, it had been her husband's suggestion for her to paint the picture. After considering this together, they were both of the view that by doing the painting she was giving the twins something back from her, as their mother.

How truly precious!

On another occasion, I was at a weekend conference— not as a speaker, but to support others who were there. The conference was about the loss of a child. Parents whose children had died were encouraged to share their stories that weekend. It was truly a privilege to be a part of it.

One mum, in particular, I shall never forget. She was a

slightly older lady. As soon as she began to talk, she broke down in tears. Eventually, she got herself together and shared with us that one day her handsome, fun-loving son, who was just about to go to university, had left the house to meet his friends. He went out full of his usual good humour. Hours later, however, he was found in their garage, having hanged himself.

This woman had been racked with guilt for eight years, she divulged, because she felt that she should have picked up on the fact that he was so unhappy. If only she had realised, she could have saved him.

She then admitted that although she still loved him so much and missed him every single day, she couldn't stop being angry at him for walking out of their lives, knowing what his death would mean to herself and his father. Her marriage had suffered, she continued, because both she and her husband found it impossible to talk about their son, due to her anger whenever his name was mentioned. One moment he was there. The next he was gone. At least if he had been ill, like the children of most others who had shared that weekend, they would have been able to hold him, and say goodbye. He had deliberately walked away, knowing they would never see him again.

And she could never forgive him for that.

She was such a dear lady. She was so honest as she confided to us that even at his funeral, which they had made as simple as possible, her anger had spilled over.

All of a sudden, she was sobbing. Most of us in the room were reduced to tears at her obvious pain and distress. She wanted now to tell him how much she loved him, she sobbed. How she was sorry if, in any way, she had failed him. Instead of the cold service they had held, she wanted to go back and do it differently.

But it was too late.

There was so much love in the room for that lady. As she began to calm down, the leader of the group asked me if I would share Grace's story. I had not intended to do this at that conference, and wondered at the appropriateness of it. Nevertheless, the leader encouraged me to contribute in this way. When I came to the end, several others told their stories, and there was helpful discussion and support from the conference leaders.

The following day was busy, with different sessions going on, and individual support being offered. We had a final lunch together, and everyone began to leave. As I was helping pack up some of the books and equipment from the weekend, I was aware of someone standing by my side.

It was the lady who had shared about her son.

'Hi, Babs,' she greeted me, with a lovely smile on her face. 'I'm leaving now, but I just wanted to let you know before I went that tomorrow my husband and I are going to have a special day out together.

We are going to throw roses on the river.

Suddenly, we were hugging each other, crying. 'When you shared Grace's story,' she informed me, 'although it was so very different to our own, I knew that God was saying, "It's not too late for a proper goodbye. Not too late to forgive him, or yourself. You live by a river. Go do it."'

We laughed together, then, knowing that a tiny baby had touched the heart of a mother who was not her own. A mother who had then gone on to find forgiveness in her heart both for her son and for herself.

I have learned, through my own experience and that of others, that in God's eyes guilt is not an option. That is what the cross is about, after all, in that 'while we were still sinners, Christ died for us.' (Rom 5:8). When, even as Christians, we sadly still mess up, we can have the sure confidence that He is not finished with us yet, and that His work in us will continue until that day when we meet Him face to face.

In September 2006, I joined the staff of the London School of Theology as Head of Housekeeping and Pastoral

Advisor to students. During the Christmas vacation that year, one of our students, Greg, who was only 25 years old, was killed in a car accident.

This tragedy shook the entire college.

Greg, who was without doubt an exceptional young man in so many ways, was greatly loved. The following January, a beautiful service of thanksgiving for his life was held at the college. I remember Greg's father sharing that some well-meaning people had complained that it was such a waste of a life. He insisted, however, that Greg's life wasn't wasted. For he believed that Greg, in his time on this earth, had fulfilled all the things that God wanted him to do.

As I observed earlier, it isn't the length of time we are here that really counts, but what we give to others during that time, and what legacy we leave behind.

Remember the 'unfinished' symphonies?

One of the songs that we sang at Greg's service remains with me now as one of my favourites. It speaks of light where there is only darkness; hope, where hope is gone; peace, where there is fear; love, where love is undeserved; pardon from sin and freedom from guilt; strength from Christ alone; and sacrifice that leads to victory.

In the words of this one song, *In Christ* Alone, so much of my own spiritual journey, from past to present day, is powerfully and poignantly reflected.

* * * * *

And so it seems that Grace's life was not wasted.

Through her existence other lives have been touched.

In the most unexpected of ways.

21

FULL CIRCLE

Jack Frost came last night,
And light of foot and finger, as an angel in flight
Rested on my windowpane,
Leaving his signature clear and plain.
Frosted snow-flaked beauty, transcendent and frail,
Delicate as a fairy-trail.
Such fragile beauty not long to see,
As the sun shall rise, the morn to free.

Through the joy of warmth in this new day,
The wondrous image melts away.
Yet as the sunlight glistens through,
The image offers blessings new.
Beauty once seen will not depart,
But remain forever in our hearts.

In our hearts, and in our souls,
A child is born, a message told;
To share her story so unique
She came to love, to bless, to teach.
And, as the snowflakes melt away,
the beauty of this child will stay.

My Dad was right, it seems—all those years ago, when I was
but a young girl. While sitting on my bed, he said that to
appreciate the warmth and brightness of the sunshine we
had to lose the beauty of our frosted picture. God was
simply concealing one blessing, in order to share with us

another. There would now be a place for a new picture to emerge, even more precious than the last.

God had in fact given Chris and I a very different picture from the one we had expected.

A different blessing that he asked us to share with others.

Now, years later, we understood why.

Some years ago, having moved into college accommodation, we found ourselves able to acquire a delightful property in a small hamlet in the Jura, in the east of France. The land around the house has an abundance of fir trees. There are three in particular that are so beautiful that whenever I sit out on the patio—enjoying the sunshine in the summer, or wrapped up warm on a frosty winter's day —I enjoy simply looking at them.

One fir tree Chris, myself, Katie, and Ben planted a few Christmases ago, for Grace. Over the years, the little Christmas fir has grown. Every year, we look forward to seeing the bright, green buds appearing on it.

Gazing on the trees, I am often reminded of a beautiful children's story that I first heard many years ago but that still carries a profound message that is as pertinent as ever.

It is called *The Three Fir Trees*.

There were three baby fir trees growing in a beautiful forest. One day, they were having a conversation about what they would like to be when they grew up.

The first fir tree was rather full of himself and declared that he wanted to be chopped down, then carved into an exquisite baby's cradle, for a royal baby to sleep in. And lots of special visitors would come and visit the child, and admire him.

The second, very pompous fir tree, said that he wanted to be chopped down and made into a grand sea-faring ship for important people to sail across the sea. As they sailed, he would hear them telling wonderful stories.

The third, very humble fir tree, observed, 'Well, I don't want to be chopped down at all. I just want to stand here, and grow tall and strong. And when people visit the forest, they will stand beneath my branches, and look up. All that I want to do is to point people to God.'

The years passed.

All three fir trees grew to become very fine trees indeed.

One day, they heard the woodcutter coming to chop them down. The first tree was very excited when he saw the woodcutter coming to him. The tree was chopped down and taken to the carpenter's shop. However, before long he was shouting, 'No! No! This is not right. I am supposed to be carved into a beautiful, exquisite cradle for a royal baby to sleep in. What's happening?' He then realised that he had been made, not into a cradle, but into a crude manger for the cows to eat out of. He was placed, not in a beautiful bedroom, but a in a smelly stable.

The tree made a lot of fuss, until someone finally came. It was a young man and woman called Mary and Joseph. On that night, their baby, Jesus, was born. He was placed in the manger. Some time later, visitors came, bearing wonderful gifts. Among them were three kings. The fir tree was very humbled when he realised that he had in fact had his wish, albeit in a different way from what he had expected.

For he did indeed hold a royal baby: Jesus, the King of kings.

Some years later, the woodcutter came again to the forest. This time, it was the second fir tree's time to be cut down. He was taken to a carpenter's shop where the carpenter began to cut, and chisel, and bang in nails. Suddenly, the tree cried out, 'Hey, wait a minute. This is not right.' He realised that he was in fact not being carved to be part of a grand sea-faring ship, but into a humble fishing boat, in which smelly fish would be carried. The tree was horrified. He sat in the carpenter's shop for many days, feeling sorry for himself.

Then, one day, he was dragged down to the water's edge. Before long, he could hear voices. A group of fishermen was approaching. 'Here we go,' he thought. 'Smelly fish.' But a man got into the boat with some of the fishermen. He sat down and started to teach them the most wonderful stories that the fir tree had ever heard. The fir tree realised that his wish had been fulfilled, although things had turned out differently to what he had expected.

He became so thankful as he grasped that he was carrying the most important person of all: Jesus.

A few years later, the third fir tree heard the woodcutter coming. 'He can't be coming for me,' he thought to himself. 'I'm not going to be chopped down. For I am going to stand here and point people to God.' 'There must have been a terrible mistake,' he cried out as the woodcutter began to swing his axe. However, the woodcutter did chop down the beautiful tree and he was taken away. A little while later, the carpenter came, and the tree thought to himself, 'Oh well, there's nothing I can do. At least I'm sure to be carved into something nice.'

As the carpenter began to hack, and cut, and carve away at the tree, his hope turned to despair as it dawned on him exactly what he was being made into. When the work was completed, he was a rough, cruel cross: a Roman gallows. He was eventually taken to a place called Calvary, and on him Jesus, the Son of God, was crucified. Through the horror of it all, the tree saw that, in the most unexpected of ways, his wish had come true.

For, as Jesus hung upon the tree, His crucifixion, His death on the cross, was the supreme means of pointing people to God.

Whenever I look at my three fir trees, I am reminded, through that children's story, that life doesn't always turn out in the way we think it will.

Nevertheless, I am reminded, too, that God's purposes are being worked out in our lives, albeit at times in quiet, even surprising ways.

So, as I watch Grace's little tree growing taller and stronger, I find true comfort, and real joy, in the consciousness that she came into our lives to be a part, with us, of pointing people to God.

She reminds us:
that memories are precious, and should be treasured, and shared;
that guilt need never be an option;
that it's never too late to grieve;
and that there is no life, however brief, that is not valued by, and special to God.

I was once given some words that were attributed to Patch Adams, the innovative American doctor whose story and methods were brought to the world's attention through the film bearing his name. He experienced real grief in his own life. This ultimately inspired him to do the work that he is now involved in.

'All of life is a coming home. All of the restless and grieving hearts of the world, all trying to find their way home. Grief: it's hard to describe what it feels like. Picture yourself in a storm of driving snow. You don't even notice that you're walking in circles, and you feel the heaviness of your legs as you trudge through the deep drifts. Your shouts disappear into the wind. How small you feel, and how far away home can be. The storm is all in your mind. Or, as Dante's poem puts it, 'In the middle of the journey of my life, I found myself in a dark wood, for I had lost the right path.' Eventually I would find it again, and in the most unlikely place.'

I have learned so many wonderful lessons over the years that have accompanied me on my own journey of grief. When I eventually broke through that grief, it was like coming home.

Yet to a home that I had never understood before.

To a place of peace and safety, after a long and lonely journey.

When friends, old and new, come to visit us, they will sometimes stand and look at Grace's embroidery. And sometimes they will say, 'Tell us about Grace.'

So I do.

> *People were bringing little children to Jesus for him to place his hands on them, but the disciples rebuked them. When Jesus saw this, he was indignant. He said to them, "Let the little children come to me, and do not hinder them, for the kingdom of God belongs to such as these. Truly I tell you, anyone who will not receive the kingdom of God like a little child will never enter it." And he took the children in his arms, placed his hands on them and blessed them.*

(Mark 10: 13-16)

It has been my privilege to share Grace's story with you.

Thank you for taking the time to read it.

Postscript

On December 27th, 2009 my Mum was called home to be with her Lord Jesus, whom she loved so dearly. She was taken suddenly ill and had been in hospital for a week. She was such a precious lady. All those who loved her were naturally devastated by the loss. Not least my dear Dad, who had loved her for 70 years.

At the Thanksgiving Service for her life, I was able to share that in the final days before her death Mum's faith was at its brightest. All those who visited her, including the doctors and nurses, were touched by it. Mum knew that she was dying. Yet there was nothing to fear. She and Dad had accepted Jesus as their Lord and Saviour in their forties and had never looked back since.

Mum knew that her family would be OK—we would be there for my Dad, and each other—and that she herself was going to heaven, to finally be with her Lord. She would in fact not die, but simply close her eyes. When she opened them again, she would be with Jesus.

My Mum had blessed me in amazing ways throughout my whole life. And even on Boxing Day, as she was slipping away, she was to bless it again.

But in a way that I never expected.

It may sound strange to say that you can experience joy at such a time. Yet it was such an immense privilege to be there with her, and watch the peace of God touch her, even then, in a new way. Her courage and grace were an inspiration. Her absolute assurance of what lay ahead was a comfort to us all. Just hours before she died, with all her immediate family around her, she was singing, as best she could in her weakened state, those great hymns *Great is thy Faithfulness* and *Blessed assurance, Jesus is mine*.

I had never before seen such peace as she slipped into heaven, and into His arms.

After mum's death, I went home to London for a few days before returning for her Thanksgiving Service. We had to stop for petrol and I got out of the car for some fresh air, tears streaming down my face. Nearby the petrol station where we stopped was a hill where for a few years, at Easter time, they had planted daffodils—Mum's favourite flower. They had also placed on the hill three crosses, reminding people of the real meaning of Easter: the death and resurrection of Jesus.

Mum loved this striking visual aid. I looked over at the hill and suddenly, in the midst of the intense pain of my grief, the Lord reminded me that Mum would now have met her little granddaughter, Grace, for the very first time.

What a meeting that would be!

As I looked again, I was reminded of the words from Psalm 121 (vv. 1-2).

'I lift up my eyes to the hills—
where does my help come from?
My help comes from the Lord,
the Maker of heaven and earth.'

I still miss my mum so very much. The pain of loss is once again so hard to express in mere words.

But this I know. Both Mum and Grace are safe and whole. They are experiencing Jesus face to face.

No more pain.

Only the experience of the fullness of His love and grace that, as yet, we cannot comprehend.

We surely will, one day . . . but not yet.

A final word from the Author

My book is finally completed. I am so thankful to those of you who have taken the time out of busy lives, to buy it, and read it. My prayer is that in some way Grace's story will have touched, supported and encouraged you, while travelling your own particular life's journey.

How do I begin to thank those who, throughout the writing of this book, have loved me, cried with me, laughed with me, and encouraged me, and who, at times when I felt inadequate to the task, gave me the courage to keep going.

My thanks go, firstly, to my husband Chris, for walking with me on the journey, and without whose love I would not have survived. He has encouraged me every step of the way with the words, 'You can do this,' teaching me that courage is not the absence of fear, but allowing that fear to transfer into faith and action. On a practical level, he gave the time out of a busy schedule to proof-read my manuscript, remaining patient and long-suffering even when faced with the tedious task of correcting my grammar and punctuation Most of all I am grateful to him for being my best friend, my soul mate, and my spiritual guide—especially throughout those lonely dark days. It was a difficult journey, but we made it. Together.

Thanks, too, to my wonderful grown-up children, Katie and Ben, for believing in me and in the value of their sister Grace's story being told. The absolute faith they had in me to write the book, never wavering in their love and support, has contributed immeasurably to its completion. In addition, Ben has provided indispensable advice and support in helping to bring the book to publication.

How I wish Grace could have known her brother and sister and shared the blessing they have both been to their Dad and to me.

I take this opportunity to express my heartfelt gratitude

to my Mum and Dad for the constancy of their unconditional love over the years. They have supported me through every new adventure, as well as through every trial, always believing in me, always encouraging, always being there. They have been my inspiration throughout my life, and remain so today.

My gratitude extends also to my sister Sue, who was an amazing support to me when Grace died. She never tired of listening, which was such a gift to me. Thanks to her for crying with me, holding me, and understanding that sometimes words just aren't enough. She is the best big sister ever.

I want, finally, to offer my sincere thanks to a number of people who have contributed to, or supported me in, the publication of this book.

Firstly, George Carey who, from reading my manuscript for the first time, has blessed me by his enthusiasm, kindness, and the belief that I could trust him with Grace's story. I have been overwhelmed by his support. It has been precious, and has been tangibly demonstrated in his gracious contribution of the foreword to this book, for which I am immensely grateful.

A huge thank you also to Margaret and Maurice Dimmock who agreed to publish *Jack Frost Came Last Night* under the auspices of the Rose Education Foundation. I know they truly understand about grief and loss and I feel humbled and privileged to partner with them in offering Grace's story to a wider audience. Thanks particularly to Margaret, who, from her initial feedback after reading my manuscript, has encouraged me all the way.

To Heather Churchill and to Ruth Coffey, for taking time out of extremely busy lives to read the manuscript of this book, and to offer a response to it, I offer my grateful thanks. Ruth was the first person to read the manuscript, and her gentle and sensitive response to it encouraged me to go forward. Heather has been likewise warm and affirming in her comments and I am grateful for the generous endorsement she has provided.

To all of those, both close family (especially here Lynn, Jo and Matt) and friends, who are mentioned in the book, who have in some way contributed to it, either by their support at the time of Grace's death, or by allowing me to share their stories, thereby making them part of our journey, I offer my grateful thanks from a full heart. You have blessed me. And, I trust, all who read this book.

Last, but never least, I offer humble thanks to my Heavenly Father. During those empty days when grief seemed so overwhelming and dark, when I could hardly put one foot in front of the other, you were the light before me. Your promises, through Scripture, were a daily reminder that you would not fail me. They offered me the unwavering assurance that you loved me and that, however my circumstances may change, your love remains constant and true. And that love has sustained me and brought me through. Thank you.

> *Do you not know?*
>   *Have you not heard?*
> *The Lord is the everlasting God,*
>   *the Creator of the ends of the earth.*
> *He will not grow tired or weary,*
>   *and His understanding no one can fathom.*
> *He gives strength to the weary*
>   *and increases the power of the weak.*
> *Even youths grow tired and weary,*
>   *and young men stumble and fall;*
> *but those who hope in the Lord*
>   *will renew their strength.*
> *They will soar on wings like eagles;*
>   *they will run and not grow weary,*
>   *they will walk and not be faint.*

(Isaiah 40:28-31)

The Rose Education Foundation

The Rose Education Foundation, founded in 2007, seeks to improve and enhance the quality of life for young people and children both in the UK and abroad.

Believing education to be one of the keys to alleviating many problems facing younger generations the foundation works extensively throughout the Tees Valley in the UK offering practical and financial support to projects seeking to improve and enrich the lives of young people in their local community.

Internationally the foundation partners with The Rahab Project in Bangkok and The Pattaya Orphanage.

If you would like to discover more of what we do please visit www.rose-edfoundation.org